I0531032

THE TITLE OF THIS BOOK *Trial by Fire*, and subtitle *"The Price of a Bucket of Tomatoes,"* came from the fact that migrant laborers are paid 25 cents for a bucket of picked tomatoes. The union representing the migrant laborers wanted to get more money for each picked bucket of tomatoes for each migrant. The farmers could use machinery rather than pay the extra money for a bucket of tomatoes, so there was a stalemate.

At this point a labor union representing the migrants tried to make an issue of the accident involving thirteen migrant laborers, to bring together the migrant laborers as a group to fight the farmers. This was the situation that brought about a lawsuit involving the fire department, police department and Lieutenant Sharpe, who was in charge of the rescue scene.

Copyright © 2008 James E. Sharpe, Jr.

Second Edition 2024.

ISBN 978-1-957077-61-1

Printed, in the United States of America.

All rights reserved.

No part of this book may be reproduced or transmitted in any form or by any means, electronic or mechanical, including photocopying, recording, or by an information storage and retrieval system, except by a reviewer who may quote brief passages in a review to be printed in a magazine or newspaper, without permission in writing from the author. For information e-mail seaboots5@aol.com.

Although the author and publisher have made every effort to ensure the accuracy and completeness of information contained in this book, they assume no responsibility for errors, inaccuracies, omissions or any inconsistency herein.

Publisher's Cataloging in Publishing
Sharpe, Captain Jim (James E.)
Trial by Fire, Price of Tomatoes / by Captain Jim Sharpe
p. cm 1. Perciformes.   2. Based on a true story.   I. Title.
ISBN: 1-889895-10-5

First Edition 2008:
Editor   Lt. Jim Sharpe
Photos   Metro Dade Fire Rescue
Cover Design   Genevieve Canizares & Jim Sharpe
Preface   Lt. Jim Sharpe
Foreword   Chief Chet Burgor
Desk Top Publishing   Genevieve Canizares

Cover: Photographs for the cover were provided by Lt. Arnold Piedrahita, Jr., the Public Information Officer Media and Public Relations Bureau for Miami Dade Fire Rescue Department. The design and background by Genevieve Canizares and Lt. Jim Sharpe.

Sea Boots Charters, Inc.
Second edition publishing assistance by BookCrafters, Parker, Colorado.

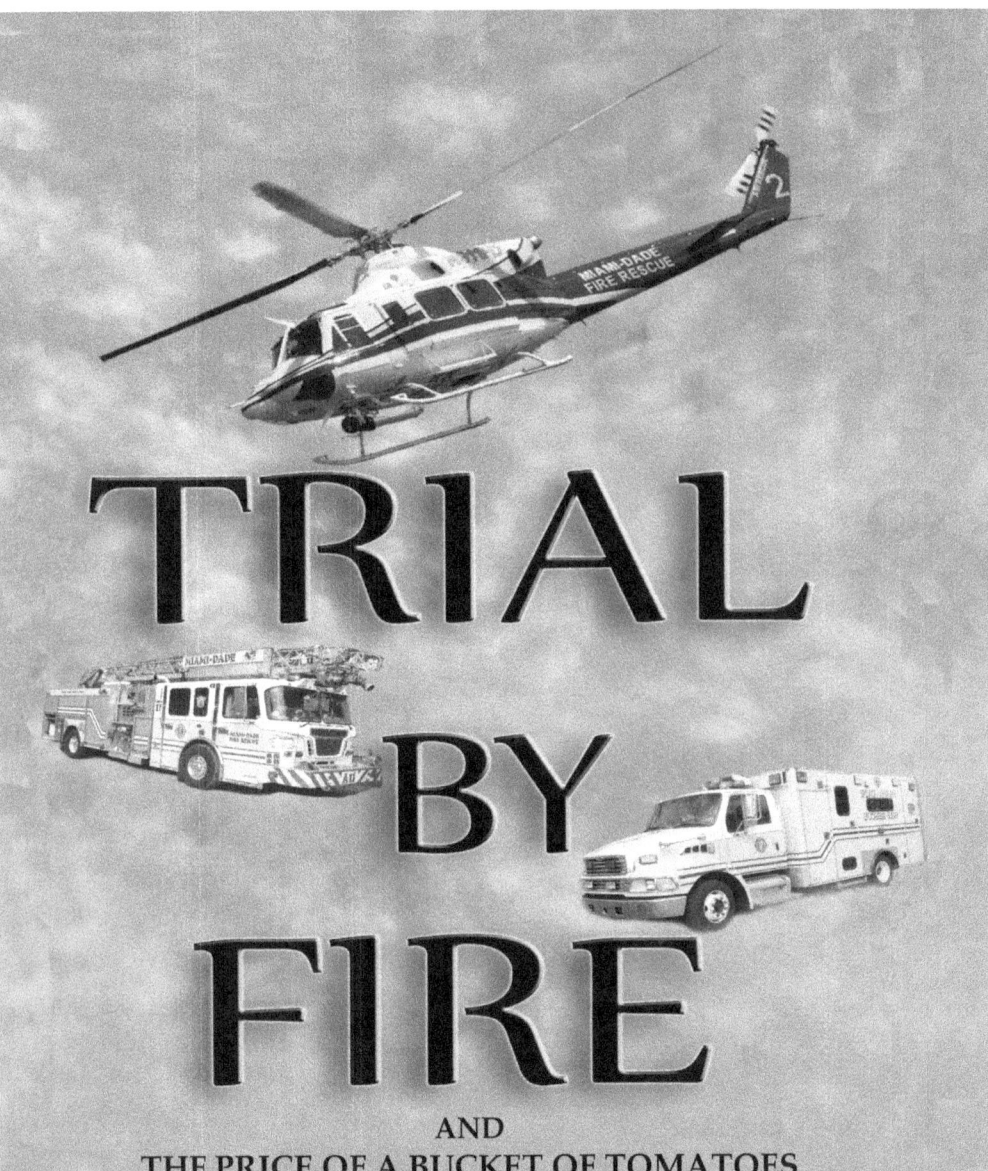

TRIAL BY FIRE

AND
THE PRICE OF A BUCKET OF TOMATOES

Lt. Jim Sharpe

TRIAL BY FIRE

AND

THE PRICE OF A BUCKET OF TOMATOES

Lieutenant Jim Sharpe

Preface

FIREMEN AND POLICEMEN belong to one of the greatest fraternities on earth. In putting on the badge, they accept the responsibility of protecting and treating all the citizens of their community. In Dade County, Florida there are approximately three million citizens, give or take a few. That is a very large responsibility when you think about it, but that is exactly why they put on the badge. To serve and protect.

It is a great feeling to know that because of your actions many people will see the dawn of the next day and be with their family. I enjoyed my twenty-eight-year career with the Fire Service and lived many happy and sad experiences. In my book, I will share many of these experiences. I was given the privilege of protecting our citizens from fires, accidents and medical emergencies. I did not expect anything in return. I accepted it as a personal challenge, but the out- pouring of respect and love from the community was overwhelming.

My reason for writing this book is to share some of my happy times, funny times and trying times with you and to stress the importance of "The Good Samaritan Act." This important Act, allows a prudent person to act to save a person's life, without fear of being sued and dragged through a court of law.

Just because the uniform hangs in the back of the closet after retirement, fireman and policeman don't change. When fireman or policeman meet after many years of not seeing each other, the conversation starts right where it left off. Sharing a lifetime of experiences makes them brothers of a very special fraternity.

Jim Sharpe

Dedication

TO THE BRAVE MEN and women of the fire and police departments that serve and protect this great country, thank you for your support. To Sonny Myers, Ron Bernstein and the staff of the Dade County Attorney's Office for their untiring efforts in defending us and educating me. To my father who I dearly loved, thank you for all the great memories of firefighting, hurricanes and fantastic fishing trips. To my mom for her love and understanding. To Frank Strahan for his guidance and the wonderful fish chowder. To my beloved wife for standing by my side through good times and bad. To my two children, Jimmy and Christina with whom I had wonderful experiences over the years.

Foreword

LIEUTENANT JIM SHARPE dedicated almost thirty years of his life to fighting fires and saving lives. He began his career as a rookie firefighter but his captain Sam Woolard quickly realized he was a very talented young man with an unstoppable drive to be the best and a quick learner.

With only a few months on the job Captain Woolard appointed him driver on a 75- foot snorkel truck. This truck weighed 35 tons and was a real challenge to drive in heavy traffic. He trained for hours learning to set up the apparatus and operate the basket. The most difficult maneuver was to raise the two-armed hydraulic platforms vertically up the side of a building, and Jim concurred it with ease. Jim drove the snorkel truck on building fires and road rescue calls. Progressing to driver engineer on Engine 19 just a couple of years into his career, he mastered hydraulics, the mathematical magic of figuring out the friction of water passing through a fire hose or standpipe system of a high-rise building to supply the right nozzle pressure for firefighting.

In 1974 he was promoted to Lieutenant and assigned the task of training engine and ladder companies on how to assist the medical rescue trucks in diagnosing and treating patients. Lt. Tyler Smith came up with a unique idea to train the firefighters at some 40 fire stations in Metro Dade County and three shifts. Tyler's unique idea was to put ten of the most experienced and knowledgeable officers on Public TV and broadcast the lessons to all 40 fire stations and the general public, on Public TV channel 2, at the same time. The idea was a huge success. All but two officers backed out due to stage fright. Lt. Dave Appleton and Lt. Jim Sharpe did the entire series. Lt. Sharpe also rode with six of the other fire departments in the area to select the best medical equipment for the new rescue trucks. The equipment consisted of EKG machines, defibrillators, med boxes, etc. After these assignments Lt. Sharpe was selected to open most of the new fire stations in the county. After opening Station 21 in Bal Harbor on Miami Beach Lt. Sharpe trained the firefighters from Bay Harbor, Bal Harbor and Surf Side on firefighting techniques in high-rise building on Miami Beach with the help of Lt. Barney Develin.

His last assignment was firefighting and rescues in rural south Dade County using the new helicopter transport system to transport trauma victims to area trauma centers.

Lt. Sharpe was considered one of the best trained and experienced Medical Rescue Officers in the country, well versed in treatment and triage in multiple victim trauma accidents in rural and high rise areas. Lt. Sharpe retired in 1993 one year after category five Hurricane Andrew, ripped through south Dade County.

Chief Chet Borger

HOW TO CONTACT THE AUTHOR

CAPTAIN JIM SHARPE writes and creates fishing books and videos. Requests for fishing information, to order books or videos should be directed to the phone and or e-mail listed below. Information about availability for seminars or Radio/TV appearances is also available at the address below.

Captain Jim Sharpe
P.O. Box 421203
Summerland Key, Fl 33042

E-mail; seaboots5@aol.com
Or
305-745-1530

COMPLETE LISTING OF BOOKS AND VIDEOS
CAN BE FOUND AT OUR WEB SITE

SEABOOTS.COM

TABLE OF CONTENTS

INTRODUCTION
TRIAL BY FIRE
AND
THE PRICE OF A BUCKET OF TOMATOES

THIS IS A STORY about the career and life of a Miami Dade firefighter/paramedic who was involved in the first civil lawsuit ever brought against a firefighter. The lawsuit revolved around an accident in deep south Dade County (Miami), where a Chevy Suburban with the driver 3.5 times legally drunk crashed the suburban into an irrigation ditch with thirteen of his family and friends in that vehicle. Four of the occupants of that vehicle were killed and nine critically injured. The people and events in this story are real, but some names were changed to protect the innocent.

Jim Sharpe, the focus of this story, comes from a family of firefighters. His uncle Frank Sharpe was the first Fire Chief at Miami International Airport and worked there for almost thirty years. His father James Sharpe retired as a captain from the City of Miami Fire Department after thirty-two years. He was called Red Sharpe, this nickname came from the fact that he had fire engine red hair and Kelly-green eyes. Another uncle, Lum Sharpe, was a firefighter in California.

Lieutenant Jim Sharpe retired after almost thirty years on the Miami Dade County Fire Department. Joining the department in 1964 and retiring in 1993 a year after Hurricane Andrew, a category five hurricane ripped through south Dade County. Jim spent most of his career working in the medical division riding rescue and fighting fires. In the Metro Dade Fire and Rescue department rescue units fight fires and the engine and ladder trucks assist with rescue assignments. Often when the senior officer is on the rescue truck, the rescue, engine and ladder trucks function as a team. In 1980 after a long and very successful career riding rescue, Lieutenant Sharpe was called to respond to an auto accident, a late-model Chevy Suburban was upside down in a drainage ditch in rural south Dade County, with 13 people trapped inside. This accident resulted in a history making lawsuit when the migrant laborers involved in the accident were convinced by a couple of Coral Gables attorneys, and a migrant organization called SALAD to sue Lieutenant Sharpe personally, the fire department, police department, landowners and the state road department. This accident happened just two weeks before the "Good Samaritan Act" was passed into law. This law would force anyone wishing to file a lawsuit to first prove negligence.

The "Spanish American League Against Discrimination" members called SALAD were active in south Dade County area at the time. They were trying to negotiate with the tomato farmers for more money for the Mexican migrants who were picking the tomatoes. The migrants were paid 25 cents for every bucket of tomatoes they picked. The problem was the farmers had equipment that could pick the tomatoes and if they paid the migrants more, it became more cost-effective to use the equipment.

The SALAD organization brought a lot of attention to the incident and tried to use this tragic accident to band the migrant laborers together to fight the farmers for more money. The ensuing media attention was like blood in the water and began to draw sharks. These sharks were dressed in nice suits and called themselves lawyers. Bertha Cruz, some months later, filed a civil lawsuit with the help of several Coral Gables attorneys, personally against four members of the Dade County Police Department, two members of the Dade County Fire Department, the State Road Department and owners of the land (were the drainage ditch was located). This civil suit was in the courts for more than three years before it was resolved. In the courtroom, history making mathematical formulas and calculations on skid marks, expert witnesses, good discovery process and the drama of a dramatic rescue deep in rural South Dade County farmland, make this a book you will not put down and will long remember.

Miami Fire Station Five located at Twentieth Street and Seventh Avenue in the City of Miami

Chapter One
GROWING UP IN MIAMI

Captain James Edward "Red" Sharpe

At the age of seven I would walk to Miami Fire Department Station Five, located at northwest 20th Street and Seventh Avenue to watch TV. I was allowed to watch "The Lone Ranger" that came on at 7:00 p.m. I was also allowed to have a moon pie and a RC Cola. My father, Captain James Edward "Red" Sharpe was in charge of the station. If a call came in while I was there, they would lock up the station and leave me inside. I will never forget the Dalmatian dog that would run and jump up on to the hose bed of the fire truck when the alarm bell signaling a fire call would sound. After the Lone Ranger was over, I would walk home only a few blocks away. That was Miami in the late 1940s. You would not even think of allowing a young person to walk anywhere in Miami a few years later. Station Five was one of the busiest fire stations in Miami at that time.

I remember years later one of the firemen telling me how he went to my father and said, "I cannot take any more smoke and fire." I guess I am just not tough enough to be a fireman. My father told him that week had been one of the worst weeks for fires he had ever seen. If he could just tough it out for a few more days, it would get better. Well, it didn't get any better but thirty years later he was still a Miami Fireman, telling me this story. In those days, firemen had no self-contained breathing apparatus to protect them from the acrid smoke and heat. I often heard it said, "In the old days ladders were made of wood and the men were made of steel."

My father "Red Sharpe" joined the Miami Fire Department in 1920 after working for the Atlanta Fire Department for a year and retired in 1952. During World War II about

1942 my father tried to join the armed services but was too old. The Coast Guard was eager to enlist him to train young service men to fight fires so he joined the Coast Guard. After several months of training fire fighters, he managed to work his way into a position running a 100-foot yacht called the "Black Swan." Their responsibility was to patrol the South Florida and Florida Keys coastline for German submarines. He had a crew of three men including himself, Buddy Carrie and Tommy Gifford. They were armed with a M-1 rifles and a 45-caliber handgun. If a sub was spotted, they would radio in and duck behind the reef.

Buddy was the son of a charter captain and fisherman in Miami at Pier Five. His father's boat was the *Bahama Mama*. Buddy would later become one of the most respected Charter Fishing Captains in the world. His boat was the *Sea Boots* and docked at Pier Five in Miami. Tommy, also a fisherman by nature, would also become one of the best-known captains fishing for giant game fish. Tommy Gifford fished all over the world and docked his boat at Ocean Reef in Key Largo in the Florida Keys. By now you are beginning to figure out how I became a fireman, joined the Coast Guard, earned a Master Captain's License and presently I am operating a charter boat by the name of *Sea Boots* on Summerland Key just north of Key West in the Florida Keys. My father saw many changes in Miami, as it evolved from a sleepy little fishing town to a large international city with a very diverse population.

My father always wanted to live in the Florida Keys. The Miami Fire Department Benevolent Association purchased a large piece of property on Key Largo. On this property they built a clubhouse, bar and restaurant and about ten small cabins for the firemen to use. While working at the firehouse, my father and a group on the firemen built ten small boats with inboard engines to be used at the property. These 16-foot boats were powered with Onan water cooled engines and were for the use of fire department families staying in the cabins. The cabins were located around a small cove with a dock on the open bay. This bay was called Barnes Sound and was attached to Black Water Sound on the Florida Bay side of Key Largo. Both of these small sounds were lined with mangrove islands and the deep channels next to the islands were filled with mangrove snapper.

Vegetation from the mangrove trees would fall and rot. This tannic acid action eroded the bottom around the islands leaving a channel right next to the island perfect habitat for the snappers and bait fish. You dared not get too close to the islands even in the daytime because the mosquitoes would literally cover your arms and legs. The time frame was late 1940s and early 1950s. In those days they didn't spray for mosquitoes.

I was about five or six years old, and I was allowed to swim in the cove. I can still remember watching all the little bait fish with a face mask. Occasionally a horse fly would bite a chunk out of your back. The snappers were not as smart back in those days as they are now, we used a cane pole with number five wire to catch the snappers. In the deep turtle grass out in the middle of the bay there were lots of sea trout. Most of the trout ranged from 2 to 4 pounds. The best bait was a shrimp on a floating bobber called a popper. If you jerked the float it would pop, sounding like a fish striking and attracting the trout. I will always remember driving down the Keys south of Key Largo as you begin to cross the bridges linking the islands together. The Atlantic Ocean was located on the left of the road and Florida Bay and the Gulf of Mexico on the right. The water was blue and clear and the sunlight danced off the water like diamonds. If you stopped at the foot of one of the bridges, hundreds of brightly colored tropical fish could be seen darting in and out of the rocks. The old bridges were very narrow, these bridges were built on top of the old railroad.

The railroad was blown out in the Hurricane of 1935; they didn't use names for the hurricanes in those days. Henry Flagler began extending the railroad from Miami to Key West in 1900 and completed the job reaching Key West in 1912. A very interesting book is titled *The Last Train to Paradise*, and although meant to be an autobiography of Henry Flagler, it details the building of railroad and their encounters with hurricanes.

My father fished in the Keys for many years and after his retirement he lived and fished from his boat the *Zipper* a good portion of the year in the Keys. He commercial fished for king fish in the winter and yellow tail and snapper in the summer. When I was about ten, I would ride the Greyhound Bus from Miami down to Marathon in the Keys to join my father and help him fish.

Marathon was a very small fishing village in those days with several fish houses and one restaurant and one store. The restaurant was named Hall's. It had a number of rocking chairs on the open front porch and the fisherman would sit and talk about the day's fishing after the meal. The store was called Cash and Carry, and it meant just that. Bring cash and carry the groceries home. In those days the shrimp boats would bring their catch into Marathon and we would get a big bucket of shrimp and several of the fishermen would get together and make a shrimp gumbo or chowder on one of the boats. The ingredients in the chowder were shrimp, lots of onion, celery, carrots, potatoes and rice. Lots of pepper and spices. On other nights it would be whatever was caught that day: snapper, grouper or cobia. The king fish would only sell for 10 cents a pound, but you could catch 500 to 800 pounds of king fish a day using wire handlines. The king fish were weighted in across the dock and loaded into tractor trailer trucks for the long ride to Miami. In those days the fish house would not even buy wahoo. Wahoo is now one of the top sellers. Years ago, fish was grossly overcooked and the wahoo would turn into leather. With today's newer techniques the delicate meat of the wahoo is preserved and prized.

After unsuccessful attempts to convince my mother to live in the Keys, my father settled on the west coast of Florida. After my father retired from the Miami Fire Department in 1952, my family moved to Punta Gorda on the west coast of Florida for a short time. Punta Gorda is located about eighteen miles north of Fort Myers on Highway US #41. We still owned a home in Miami at Twelfth Street and Seventh Court. The property my father purchased on the west coast was located on Alligator Creek and all 20 Acres were waterfront. This was a dream come true for me. This creek some 75-feet wide and 10-foot deep was teaming with snook, sugar shad, sheep head and big black mullet. At the east end of the property was a dam and above that was all fresh water with lots of gar fish, brim and bass. My father built a CBS home on the property and we had well water.

Hurricanes were always taken very seriously in our home. My father was a fireman in Miami when the 1926 hurricane devastated Miami. He was in charge of the first rescue team to enter the Keys after the 1935 Hurricane, and I still remember the stories of people washed into the ocean and dead bodies piled up and burned where the Hurricane Monument stands today in Islamorada. I remember my father talking about the *Miami Herald* Newspaper hitting the streets the night before the hurricane of 1926. The headline read "Minor Hurricane Brushes Miami with Little or No Damage." The newspaper was trying to not scare off tourists by minimizing the hurricane, but in fact Miami was devastated by a major hurricane. A 200-foot ship was washed up on to the land in downtown Miami and became a restaurant and later an aquarium. Miami Fire Station One was located where the Federal Building is today in downtown Miami and had four feet of water inside from the tidal surge. Thankfully my father's experience with hurricanes prepared me for my experiences with hurricanes that were yet to come.

My father passed away at age 58 of a heart attack in 1960. His passing left a very large void in my heart. When we were going fishing, whether off Miami or the Keys I didn't have to worry about waking up early, I never went to sleep. One of our old family friends, Frank Strahan and his family would join us on many of those fishing trips. Frank was an attorney in Miami and had a very large family of five kids. Frank's passion was sailing and sailboats. When my father's boat the Zipper, a 34-foot Bacus Hull built in Palm Beach would break down, and it often did, Frank was in his glory. He would rig a sail and sail the boat back into the bay where they could find a tow back to the dock. Frank's specialty was fish chowder; it was spicy hot and delicious. Plenty of bread and butter was needed to put out the fire. Frank's family and ours made many trips to the Keys, usually to Marathon. Frank was always late whenever we were going somewhere. My father said he would be late for his own funeral.

We always had a great time; first the toilet on the boat would stop up, then the motor would act up, then we would anchor for the night and dive up fresh Florida Lobster for dinner and catch some yellow tail snapper. Frank had a special way of cooking the fish. He would remove the head, guts and scales leaving the tail on. Then he would pass a piece of wire through the tail of several of the whole fish and lower them down into a boiling pot of cooking oil. These yellow tails were small, about ten inches in length, and he would cook them until they looked like fried chicken. I'm telling you, they would melt in your mouth. After my father passed away, Frank and I fished together a number of times. I still see his kids and we occasionally fish together.

Chapter Two
A FIRE DEPARTMENT CAREER BEGINS

In 1964 I applied for a job with the Miami Fire Department but was turned down on the medical because my father died of a heart attack at age 58, even though it was eight years after he retired. I was hired by the City of North Miami Fire Department a smaller department just north of Miami. In 1969 North Miami Fire Department was taken over by Dade County Fire Department, later to be known as Miami Dade Fire and Rescue. At this point I had reached my goal, belonging to a large, very busy and very professional fire department.

Opportunities for advancement were endless. The rescues were handled by ambulance services from 1969 to 1974. Miami Dade Fire and Rescue covered some 2000 square miles of high-rise building, farming areas, industrial areas and residential homes and apartments. We had to cover a vast amount of territory with just a few units, this meant longer response times and bigger fires. Dade County was growing so fast that fire inspectors could not keep up with preventing fires.

A good fire prevention program can limit the number of serious fires. From 1969 to 1974 I was a driver engineer. This is the best job on the fire department. I was stationed at northwest 132nd Street and 7th Avenue on Engine 19. This American La France unit was capable of pumping 1200 gallons of water a minute, one of the largest in the county. Our location was close to the old wood- frame houses of the northwest section, business and industrial areas, and the high-rise apartments on the bay. Needless to say, we were very busy fighting fires. We handled seven civil riots in those years. Civil unrest would explode into rioters setting fire to everything in their neighborhood, even local businesses. In one of these riots nineteen people were killed, and 100 million dollars' worth of businesses were destroyed in just three days.

In time the local leaders learned how to prevent these senseless riots. In 1974 I was promoted to lieutenant and was assigned to survey all of the medical equipment being used by other fire department rescues in the area. I was one of the few members of the department that had prior medical experience. While working for North Miami Fire Department I rode rescue. In the city, the City Doctor responded with the rescue trucks and there was not much we couldn't do.

The Metro Dade Fire Department was adding rescue trucks and a Medical Division. I was assigned to evaluate the medical equipment being used by other fire departments and recommended equipment for Metro Dade's Rescue Trucks. It was a great experience riding with all the different Fire and Rescue Departments in our area. I rode with Miami Beach Fire and Rescue, Hialeah Fire and Rescue, North Miami Beach Fire and Rescue and the City of Miami Fire and Rescue. I rode Rescue One in downtown Miami with the City of Miami Fire Department.

The Captain on the truck was Randy Boaz, he worked as a rookie under my father when he first came on the Miami Department. That morning at Miami's Station One while helping to check out the equipment and drugs, I noticed the far wall in the apparatus floor had a number of plaques with names on them. One of the plaques read Captain James E. Sharpe, I was confused at first, then realized that was my father's plaque. Although this was a new station, built long after my father retired and had passed away, they were still honoring their retirees.

On our first call out of the station Randy insisted I sit in the front jump seat. I was treated like an honored guest. The firemen on the City of Miami Fire Department were gentlemen and very professional. I cannot say that for all the departments I rode with. When I rode with North Miami Beach Fire and Rescue, it was a different story. The first morning I walked into the station, one particular Captain decided that I was going to mop the floor. Now I have no problem with mopping floors, but generally speaking, officers assign tasks, not mop floors. I told this particular Captain that I would be glad to help him mop the floor, but he would have to join me. When he again decided to order me to mop the floor, I didn't say anything.

I just walked into to his Chief's office, who I knew quite well, and asked him if he wanted me to mop floors. After all, that was not why I was assigned there. This Captain suddenly became very friendly when I addressed his Chief by his first name, Stanley. What followed was a fairly rough attitude adjustment by the Chief on the Captain.

After this brief but painful encounter, I walked out to the apparatus floor where this young firefighter by the name of David Paulson was checking out the equipment on the rescue truck. David was a breath of fresh air, and very knowledgeable and eager to demonstrate the rescue equipment and point out the good and bad points of each piece of equipment. This was exactly the kind of information I needed so I could advise our medical team on what to purchase for our trucks. As it turned out, a few years later North

Miami Beach was taken over by our department Miami Dade Fire and Rescue. David Paulson later worked his way up through the ranks to become the Chief of Miami Dade Fire and Rescue.

After retiring he was appointed to the head of Homeland Security where he was working at the time of this writing. I knew David was going places from the first day I met him, and it couldn't happen to a nicer guy.

Chapter Three
BUILDING A NEW FIRE RESCUE DIVISION

Miami Dade Fire and Rescue was building a brand-new rescue division and wanted the best and most modern equipment available. The department underwent a massive reorganization and training mission. Engine and ladder companies needed to be trained to assist the new rescue units, setting up IV's and drips, recognizing drugs and equipment such as a defibrillator, EKG machine, Thumper or MAST suit, etc. Our Rescue Paramedics received the best medical training in the world. Most were trained at Jackson Memorial Hospital at the University of Miami, Doctors Labs in Miami, Mount Sinai and Miami Heart Institute. Little did I know that I would need all this training and more to protect myself and my assets later in a court of law.

One of our more progressive training officers, Tyler Smith, came up with a great idea. Several of the rescue officers with prior experience and training in the medical field would each take a section; heart attacks, strokes, pediatric emergencies, trauma, etc. and conduct a class on Public Service Television (Channel Two).

He instructed the engine and ladder companies on how to recognize medical emergencies and to assist the medical rescue units when they arrive. In this way we could reach all thirty stations via TV at one time. We put this program together and presented it to the top brass in the department. They gave us the OK but wanted nothing to do with it. When the televised training began, we had ten paramedics to teach the classes. Unfortunately, when they saw the size of the camera in the TV studio, eight of them backed out. The old TV cameras looked like a 105 Howitzer cannon mounted on a crane.

After the dropouts, Lieutenants Dave Appleton and Jim Sharpe did all the sections. When the top brass figured out that two million taxpayers and all the fire companies were tuned into this training on public television, they had a sudden change of heart and became involved. Wild horses could not keep them away now. These training classes were a bigger hit with the general public than with the fire houses.

After countless hours of training in medical emergencies, one fact was driven home time and time again, "experience is the best teacher." In Dade County experience came with the territory, covering over 2000 square miles of high-rise residential properties, rural farmland, economically depressed areas and a vast cultural diversity. I stopped counting my child deliveries at 200. The diversity of the calls was as diverse as the territory itself; airplane crashes, high-rise building fires, auto accidents, farm accidents, industrial accidents, grass fires, medical calls--every call added to your experience.

Some rescues called for imagination. One of our rescue units was called on to start an IV in a vein under a tiger's tong. The tiger (unconscious) was the victim of a poisonous boffo frog that he tried to eat. The rescue crew injected a large amount of atropine to counteract the poison. The tiger did fine. On another day one of our rescue units was dispatched to a call at the Miami Serpentarium where a young baby accidentally fell into a pit with two 18-foot Indian crocodiles, one of the crocodiles quickly grabbed the child and sank to the bottom of the pit. Rescue Four arrived and jumped into the pit and began punching the crocodile with a pike pole. A long pole with a medal end for pulling down ceiling after a fire. The crock released the baby, but unfortunately it was too late. Oddly a young boy nine-years-old at the time, witnessed the actions of the firefighters and was so impressed he joined the department some twelve years later. This young man was relating the story at the fire house while eating supper one day only to discover the Captain at the end of the table was the officer in the pit with the crocodile. Captain Frank "Catfish" Spadaro. The Spadaro brothers were all dedicated firefighters Nino, John and Frank and good friends.

Metro Dade Air Rescue Two

Chapter Four
FIRES AND RESCUES ON MIAMI BEACH

I spent a large portion of my career on Miami Beach, my territory was from 85th Street to 217th Street. South of 85th Street was covered by Miami Beach Fire Department. This area was mostly high-rise apartments and hotels with some of the oldest and wealthiest residential areas in the state: Indian Creek, Bal Harbor, Bay Harbor and Golden Isles. In these neighborhoods the doctor comes to the house with all necessary equipment. My task in this area was to train the ladder and engine companies the methods of fighting high-rise building fires and rescues. These large buildings and areas inside or behind the structures required lots of manpower to bring all needed equipment to the scene.

This area was bordered on the east by the Atlantic Ocean and on the west by Biscayne Bay. In other words, we were surrounded by water, boats, docks and beaches.

Miami Dade Fire and Rescue took over the Bal Harbor, Bay Harbor and Surfside Fire Departments in 1974. I had just been promoted to Lieutenant and was stationed at Bal Harbor that was Station 21. We were housed in the Bal Harbor Police Station on the second floor. Our fire equipment consisting of a American La France 100-foot ladder truck and medical rescue truck were housed on the ground floor. We also had a station in Surfside about one-half mile south with an engine company. Many of the firefighters that were employed by the area prior to our takeover of the departments were retired firefighters from big city departments like New York. Older firefighters, but very knowledgeable, could still get the job done.

In 1970 prior to the Metro Dade take over, Barney Devlin a retired firefighter from

New York, along with his driver engineer, and one tail board man extinguished a major fire in the basement of the Americana Hotel at 96 Street and Collins. Basement fires are one of the hardest fires to extinguish, you must go down and heat comes up, not good. Barney was a grizzly old firefighter working 27 years on a ladder truck in New York, I don't think there is much he has not done. When the mutual aid companies from Miami Beach arrived they could not believe that Barney and his nozzle man had extinguished that basement fire.

Fires and rescues on Miami Beach were difficult due to the large buildings and heavy traffic conditions. Right after I was assigned to Station 21, then located in the Bal Harbor Police Station, we received a call to a very large Five and Dime Store located on 9445 Harding Avenue in Surfside. Rescue 21 and Ladder 21 responded as a unit, and I was the commanding officer. Engine 22 with Lieutenant Barney Devlin was responding from Surfside just 10 blocks south of the Fire and Engine 10 responded from 191st Street and Collins Avenue some 100 blocks north of the incident. Rescue 21 was just two blocks away from the incident when the alarm went out. We quickly arrived at the front of the building. I ran inside and saw flames running up the wall from an electrical outlet inside the store. The only fire extinguisher in the store was empty, I sent my crew to the rescue for an extinguisher, I contemplated filling my fire helmet with water from a nearby sink to extinguish the small fire but thought better of the idea due to the electrical nature of the fire.

The fire was advancing quickly, and I made sure all the customers and store clerks were out of the store and bathrooms. My crew came busting through the door with the extinguisher, but it was too late. The fire had quickly spread into the area above the false ceiling and began to flash over, catching all the stock on the top shelves on fire. Using my hand-held radio, I informed the alarm office we had a code one and would possibly go to a second alarm. A code one is a working fire where all of the dispatched units on the first alarm will be engaged in fighting the fire, the second alarm would bring additional firefighting units to the scene.

Automatically on a code one additional equipment would begin moving to the vacated stations (termed a move up). These units would protect the area and become the second alarm assignment if needed. Engine 22 and Ladder 21 arrived at the front door and began to fight the now fully involved store with four 1½ jump lines, each of these lines deliver 90 gallons of water a minute and are very mobile. Engine 10 arrived at the back door and began fighting the fire with a B-800 delivering 300 gallons a minute. Engine 18 arrived on the second alarm and laid two lines in from a hydrant and supplied Engine 22 and Ladder 21. Engine 11 laid two lines in the rear of the building and supplied Engine 10. The quick action of these fire crews extinguished the fire quickly and saved the stores on either side of the Five and Dime Store. I had fought many fires, but this was my first experience standing there watching how quickly this fire advanced.

My advice is, if you are in a store with a heavy fire load like a five and dime or drug store and a fire starts, leave on a dead run and don't look back. In that same block we had a fire in a restaurant, we quickly extinguished the fire and began to ventilate. One of the workers had apparently gone back into the restaurant looking for something and died of smoke inhalation. Our rescue attempts were in vain. Do not go back in unless you have a self-contained mask and hose line!

Chapter Five
RIP CURRENTS AND UNDERTOW
ON HAULOVER BEACH

Most of the area on the beach from 85th Street north to the Dade County line was swimming beaches. Unfortunately, most of the swimmers were from out of town and not at all familiar with the dangers of rip currents and undertow. When the wind comes from an offshore direction, northeast or east, it can create a very dangerous condition called rip currents and undertow along the beaches. The mechanics of these currents are fairly simple: the offshore wind drives the sea water onto the beach, as the tide rises on the incoming tide. The sand along the beach moves with the wave action of strong offshore winds often building up a shallow sandbar 20 to 40 feet offshore. This sandbar is under the water with two to three of water over it, as you travel toward the beach it gets deeper perhaps four to five feet of water. The water continues to build on to the beach with the offshore wind and rising tide until the sandbar blows out. This creates a small opening or channel through which the water flows offshore at a very fast rate of speed. Swimmers can be swept laterally down the beach then offshore with the rushing water. The lateral movement is called undertow and moves toward the channel and the offshore movement a rip current.

This is a very dangerous situation and has been responsible for hundreds of drownings along Miami Beach, particularly along the northern end of the beach where there are fewer lifeguards. During my years on the northern end of the beach we would get alarms with as many as twenty swimmers in near drowning situations. The lifeguards on the beach deserve a lot of credit for saving thousands of lives. I have witnessed lifeguards place themselves in one of these offshore currents and try to swim against it. Even highly trained exceptionally strong swimmers were no match for a rip current. The proper way to save your life is to not try and swim against the current, swim laterally across the current until you are out of the current, then swim to the beach. Of course, this takes a very strong swimmer. An even better solution would be to obey the danger signs of rip currents and not go into the water. Usually warning signs are posted on the beach.

We worked many drowning victims from these currents, sometimes multiple victims. There is a fundamental difference between a saltwater drowning victim and a fresh water drowning victim. In the case of a fresh water drowning victim (pool, etc.) a small amount of water enters the lungs. The osmotic pressure difference between fresh water and the plasma in the alveoli (small cells in the lung that exchange oxygen) results in fresh water passing through the alveoli into the plasma and diluting the plasma (blood). This dilution results in red blood cells being distorted and not being able to carry oxygen to the cells. This makes fresh water drowning more difficult to manage than saltwater drowning.

In the case of a saltwater drowning, that small amount of saltwater enters the lungs and the difference in osmotic pressure allows plasma to flow into the lungs through the alveoli. This fluid or plasma in the lungs is termed pulmonary edema, often the cause of death in smoke inhalation, heart attacks and saltwater drowning victims. However, fluid in the lungs can be forced back into the arteries and out of the lungs by several means. In the rescue truck when working a saltwater drowning victim we would immediately use rotating tourniquets and pressurized oxygen delivered by mask. Rotating tourniquets are large elastic rubber bands that are placed on three extremities. Usually both legs and one arm to start, then rotated every fifteen minutes. This in conjunction with the pressurize oxygen delivered by mask will begin to force plasma out of the lungs and trap it in the extremities and assist the alveoli in exchanging oxygen. This is mechanical and can be done immediately while an IV is established on the patient. Once the IV is established, 75 milligrams of LASIK are administered IV push and followed by a drip. It's a good idea to strap drowning victims to the stretcher, because if they were in cardiac arrest or anoxic for a period of time low levels of oxygen in the brain can cause them to be violent as they regain oxygen. Many of our drowning victims were in cardiac arrest when we received them from lifeguards. In this event we would defibrillate the victim to try and establish a heart rate.

One mistake you don't want to make is defibrillating a victim while kneeling in wet sand; take them well up the beach to dry sand. I made that mistake once it will not happen again. Being hit with 400-watt seconds of electricity is a sobering experience, kind of like being hit by a Mack truck. No wonder my patients balked when I was using cardioversion on them, that's only 50-to-100 watt seconds. All near drowning victims should be watched closely for several days after the incident. They can crash very suddenly.

Chapter Six
FIRES AND RESCUES
IN HIGH-RISE BUILDINGS

On a rescue on the beach behind a hotel we would load our stretcher with all needed equipment because it was an 800-foot trip through the building if you forgot something. High-rise building fires were even more demanding and required lots of manpower. Station 21 located first in the Police Department Building in Bal Harbor was later moved to Haulover Inlet. In this area the population was elderly, 68 percent were over 65 years of age. On a busy shift, we would work as many as nine cardiac arrests in a single 24-hour shift. Working any kind of medical emergencies in high-rise building is challenging. The elevators are too small to handle stretchers with a patient on the thumper. Just capturing an elevator could be a task. We would load all of our equipment on the stretcher we thought we would need, returning to the truck for equipment was not an option.

We were responding to a heart attack in one of the Winston Towers Buildings, these are 32-story condos, and as we passed through the lobby, two elderly gentlemen were sitting on a bench. One asked me what floor we were going to on the emergency. I told him we were headed for the tenth floor. He turned to his friend a said, "There's going to be a vacancy on the tenth." We entered the elevator with the stretcher and equipment and one of the elderly gentlemen started to get on with us. I told him he would have to take the next elevator and he stepped out. The doors to the elevator closed and before we could get moving the elderly gentlemen pushed the up button on the outside. The doors opened and I asked him to please not push the button until we started up. The doors closed and again he pushed the button and the doors opened, not allowing the elevator to move.

He walked like the comedian Tim Conway on the Carroll Burnett show, so I took him by the arm and walked him down the hall about fifty feet and ran back to the elevator the doors closed and we were finally off. In this area there was never a dull moment.

A simple auto accident in one of the parking garages could turn into a major incident. A nice little lady was backing out of her parking space and accidentally hit the gas instead of the brake running over three pedestrians walking past. We arrive and the three pedestrians have serious trauma injuries. As if this is not enough, the driver suffers a heart attack right on the scene.

There were lots of rescues with lighter notes. We received a call from the alarm office that a young man had been taken out to sea on a surfboard. One of the residents in a high-rise on the beach observed the incident. This rescue was just south of the Haulover cut, strong currents and the fact that it is going to be dark in about thirty minutes brought additional urgency to the matter. On arrival we could see the young man on the surfboard, and he looked to be OK and was making his way back to the beach. I canceled the Coast Guard helicopter that had been in route. When the young man reached the beach, we could see he had a fishing pole in his hands. I inquired, what happened. He said, "Well I was fishing along the beach from my surfboard when I hooked this big tarpon, and he took me out to sea. You got to love it when there is a little humor at the end of the day.

After we moved into the new Fire Station located next to Bakers Haulover, things got a lot better. In the old Police Station in Bal Harbor we would get calls all night, usually one of the police men's wives or girlfriend. In the fire house we would sleep until a call came in, so this got to be quite a rub. We were now in the brand-new station and no more unwanted calls not relating to us.

One night about 2:00 a.m. I was awakened by the hot line. This was a phone line direct from the alarm office where rescue calls would come in during the night. This station housed a ladder truck, engine company, rescue truck and Battalion Chief. If there was a fire, the station alarm bell would be set off to awaken all companies, but on rescues we were notified by phone so not to awaken all the crews. We boarded the rescue truck and started north on Collins Avenue toward a large hotel at 163 Street and Collins Avenue. The alarm office told me on the phone the incident was a man being choked by a snake. My rescue man in the rear of the truck was a very large fireman by the name of Frank Hartley. Now Frank was deathly afraid of snakes, big or small. On the way to the rescue, Frank slid open the small window between the rear of the truck and the cab and asked what type of call we were responding to! I told him we were responding to a man being choked by a snake. Frank muttered some bad words and slammed the window shut. I guess we had kidded Frank too much with rubber snakes and real snakes.

When we arrived at the scene, we unloaded the stretcher from the back of the truck and again Frank asked what kind of call it was, and I repeated myself followed by, "I am really not kidding. A man is being choked by a snake." Frank, now slowly beginning to believe me, asked what kind of equipment should we bring. I said, well we better bring it all until we see what we will need. Oh and if you have a snake hook bring that too.

We loaded all our medical gear onto the stretcher and then led by one of the employees to a stage in the rear of the building. Frank was still muttering expletives as we walked along. Sure enough, we found a man being choked by a snake. Frank's eyes were the size of dinner plates, this was not just a snake it was an 18-foot long anaconda and weighted about 300 pounds. The man being choked was an entertainer and was putting on a night club act where he would let the snakes (two of them) wrap around him. Well one of the snakes didn't read the script. It wrapped around him and then each time he exhaled the big snake tightened up his grip until the entertainer could not expand his chest to breathe.

Several of the snake handlers worked with us to remove the snake and the victim began breathing on his own. Our patient was still a little cyanotic (blue) and we administered some high flow oxygen until he pinked up. I advised our patient that he should be checked out at a local hospital. Our victim refused any further medical help and signed off on my rescue report that he refused any further treatment. On the way back to the station Frank voiced his concern that he might be in trouble. In the fire service, a semi military organization, you don't question an officer's command or authority. I laughed and told Frank, "You are not in trouble. I guess that was payback for all the times we kidded you about snakes. This will make a great story for my grandkids someday."

Being in the fire and rescue business can bring some strange experiences, and not all are funny or rewarding. It is always rewarding to go on a call and know that if not for you and your crews medical training and intervention somebody's husband, wife, or daddy would not be going home. Then there are those calls that are just strange. Ed Kassner and I were working an overtime shift out of Station 21, on Haulover Beach in northeast Miami. It was a chamber of commerce day, bright and sunny and the ocean was as blue as the sky. Ed and I had just left the station when we received a call for a boat stranded on the beach with possible injuries near the main lifeguard stand on Haulover Beach. We were only a minute or so away, and on arrival we were met by several of the lifeguards, and they began to tell us the rest of the story.

Metro Dade Air Rescue One performing host drill

According to the lifeguards this off duty Metro Police Officer came in just 50-feet offshore in a 25-foot outboard boat. The lifeguards fearing the swimmers on the beach would be hit by the prop, yelled to him to go father offshore. The police officer then pulled a gun (pistol) and began to threaten the lifeguards while waving his police badge. The police officer lost control of the boat and ended up stranded on the beach. On our arrival the officer was just sitting in the sand about ten feet from the water with the pistol lying beside him. All the lifeguards had taken cover behind a brick wall about 100 feet from the officer. I informed the alarm office of the situation and they updated the responding police units.

When the first police unit arrived, the officer just walked down to the officer sitting in the sand and picked up the weapon. The off-duty officer offered no resistance and went quietly with the officer. Several days after this incident the officer in the sand showed up on a rescue call with us in a high-rise. The officer seemed irritated and was quite rude to the patient. I quietly informed my crew not to take issue with the officer; we would handle it later. After the call I had a conversation with the shift commander and the officer was put on inactive duty until the issues could be resolved. What the issues were I will never know, perhaps drugs if had to guess.

Chapter Seven
RUN AWAY RESCUE TRUCK

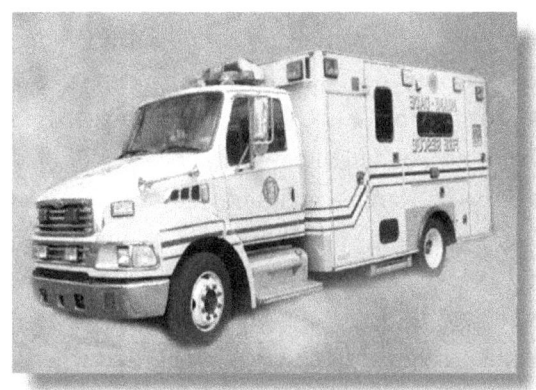

Ed Brown was my CR relief officer when I was stationed on the beach at Station 21. The CR day, or Croy Day as it was called, was designed to reduce the hours we worked each week. My CR day was on Friday, I didn't have to come to work on that day and Ed would work the shift for me. Well, it was my CR day off, and Ed was working with my regular driver Jim Merrill. It was a normally busy day; Miami Beach was known for the large number of heart attack victims. Jim and Ed (only two paramedics on the truck) had responded to a patient having chest pain in Golden Beach. Golden Beach is an affluent area on the northern end of the beach. They ran an EKG and determined the patient was in fact having a heart attack. IV with D5W was started, O2 administered, and the patient was placed on a stretcher and loaded into the rescue truck for transport to Mount Sinai Hospital on the south end of the beach.

Now I have to paint this picture carefully. Jim Merrill is the driver, and the truck is a modular. The front cab of the truck is separated from the patient compartment, there is a small sliding window in-between. Ed Brown is in the back of the truck with the patient monitoring the IV, O2 and the EKG. Heart attack patients can go down quickly and need to be monitored very carefully. Jim gets bogged down in traffic at an intersection and has to wait for the light to change before he can continue.

Ed is in the back with the patient and notices a driver in another car waving at him and motioning the compartment door on the outside of the rescue unit is open. Ed turns to Jim Merrill and tells him to stay stopped for a moment, I have to get out and close the compartment door. Ed steps out of the unit to close the door just as the traffic clears and Jim takes off through the intersection leaving Lieutenant Ed Brown standing in the middle of the street. Now Merrill is driving on a 3 signal (red lights and sirens) going down Collins Avenue toward the hospital and the patient is on the stretcher in the back of the unit with the oxygen mask on his face, IV going, not aware that all this is taking place, and he is all alone.

As Ed stood in the middle of the street, he pondered for a minute and decided he better do something quick. He flagged down a pickup truck and asked the driver if he could help him catch up to the rescue truck. The old redneck driving the truck spit out his chew and said, "Get in." Now the rescue truck is speeding south toward the hospital with the patient in the back and no paramedic. Jim Merrill is not aware of the situation in the back of the truck. Meanwhile, Lieutenant Brown is speeding through traffic in a redneck roadster (pick up) attempting to catch the rescue truck. Ed remembers he has his portable radio in his back pocket and attempts to call Merrill on the radio, to no avail. The noise from the air horns and sirens can muffle radio signals when you are running a 3 signal in traffic. Ladder 21 was doing a building inspection on Collins Avenue and heard the frantic call from Ed Brown. The ladder crew flagged down the runaway Rescue 21 with Merrill at the wheel and Ed Brown in the redneck roadster caught up. Thankfully the patient never realized the situation and was doing fine when paramedic Ed Brown climbed back into the Rescue and they continued on to the hospital.

Only Ed and the laundry man will know the real situation.

Chapter Eight
WORKING OVERTIME

During the late1970s and 1980s there was a lot of overtime work for our paramedics. It would seem we were expanding faster than we could train paramedics for the job. For officers, overtime shifts were usually tough, riding with a crew you were not used to working with and often in a strange area. I pulled a 12-hour overtime shift on Rescue Four located on US 1 Highway and 152nd Street southwest. It was a daytime shift not usually as busy as the night shift.

Station Four's area was a mixture of low-income residential homes and apartments, a large area of businesses along US 1 and some very expensive homes on the east side of the highway. During this particular shift we received a call of a young boy having a seizure at 127th Avenue and 187th Street southwest. We arrived to find a boy about ten years of age sitting on the side of the road under a shade tree. Upon evaluation I found him to be confused, he had several cut marks on his tongue and had lost his water. (urinated on himself). These are signs that the patient had in fact had a seizure, and he was not a known epileptic. We were waiting for an ambulance to arrive to transport the patient to the hospital for further evaluation. The ambulance crew arrived in just a few minutes, and I filled them in on my diagnosis.

As the ambulance crew prepared to load the patient onto the stretcher, I noticed an old white Cadillac stopped in the street directly in front of us. A man calmly got out of the car and walked to rear of the car and opened the trunk. What I saw next got my full attention, he pulled a 222 automatic assault weapon out of the trunk, released the safety and cocked the gun. He began to cuss as he pointed the riffle at my chest and exclaimed he was going to kill all of us.

Unknown to me, this person had an argument in traffic at a nearby intersection with the crew of the ambulance. I picked up on this little bit of information as the ambulance driver began once again to argue with the man with the gun. I quickly told the ambulance driver that this man was right and not to continue this argument. After all, when a man has a gun pointed at my chest it is bad manners to have a heated argument with him. The driver quickly caught on that this situation needed to be defused not agitated.

The gun man was standing on the edge of the roadway about six feet away from me. As I explored my options, I decided that I could not move quickly enough to grab the gun before he could pull the trigger. I continued to talk the gun man down agreeing with everything he said. During this confrontation I realized that the patient was directly behind me and that if the gun man did what he said he was going to do, the bullets would go through me and strike the patient. I slowly reached behind me and pulled the patient to one side in the hope that a spray of bullets would miss him.

After what seemed like an hour, but realistically was only a few minutes, I began to talk the gun man down; he seemed to lose most of that intense rage he had displayed when he first arrived on the scene. After all, I had years of training in dealing with the most intense mentally ill and diffusing the problems. The gun man and I came to an understanding that the ambulance driver was wrong and he was right, and we would just walk away from the problem. He walked slowly back to the trunk of the car and placed the riffle in the open trunk then walked to the driver's door. I walked slowly toward the car and was within striking distance when I noticed there was another man sitting in the passenger seat. I could not tell if he had a weapon or not. I decided rather than try to take the gun man out I should just stand down and let him drive away. As the gun man drove away, I stepped into the roadway and wrote the license tag number and description of the vehicle on my hand.

I pulled my portable radio from my back pocket and called the alarm office. Rescue 4 to Dade County. The alarm office responded, stand by Rescue four. Rescue 4, I have and emergency. Alarm office responded, QSK (what?). Rescue 4, we have an unknown male that threatened to kill us on our rescue scene with a 222 automatic assault weapon. No one has been shot! The gun man has just left the scene headed north on 137 Avenue in a 1960's white Cadillac with a license tag number of 4318D FL. There are two male occupants in the car and the riffle was placed in the trunk of the car when they departed the scene. I don't know if the passenger is armed or not. The driver was extremely violent and is armed and dangerous.

This report came as somewhat of a shock to the dispatcher at the alarm office, but then I always seemed to be in the right place at the wrong time. The dispatcher told me later she thought it was a joke because I was so calm. I responded, well we are trained to handle emergencies. I can tell you one thing, I thought to myself, *Only me and the laundry man will ever know how bad that situation was*. I felt that there was a fine line between the gun man walking away or him shooting everybody on the scene.

The fire alarm office and police alarm office are in the same big room and the BOLO "Be On The Look Out" when out within seconds to all the Metro Police units on patrol in the area. There was an undercover detective driving west on southwest 152nd Street just after the BOLO went out and he spotted a white Cadillac fitting the description of the BOLO parked in front of the 7/11 store at 152nd Street and US 1. The detective parked across the street and called for backup. Before the backup arrived, the two men departed the 7/11 store and proceeded west on 152nd Street with the unmarked detective's car following. The detective was able to make out the tag and it matched. The backup units began arriving behind the unmarked police car, and they prepared to stop the vehicle. In a case like this they wanted a safe place to pull the vehicle over. Before they could initiate the stop the vehicle pulled into a driveway at 103rd Avenue and 152nd Street and stopped. The police units swarmed the car, and both men were taken into custody without incident.

I was still running rescue calls when I got the call from the alarm office to meet the police at 103rd and 152nd Streets. As soon as we cleared our rescue call, we took a 10 (out of service) to meet the police to identify the subject. When we arrived at the gun man's location, I saw the familiar white Cadillac sitting in the driveway. The gun man was in the back seat of one of the patrol cars. As I walked up to the patrol car one of the officers pulled him out of the back seat and asked him to stand next to the car. To my surprise he was about five foot six in height. With the riffle in his hands standing on the upper part of the roadway, I thought he was six-foot-two, at least. There was no doubt in my mind he was the gun man. The officers upon a search of the vehicle found the 222 assault weapon in the trunk of the car. I later found out that he had just been released from a mental institution. After many visits to the State Attorney's Office, I lost tract of the disposition of the case. I don't think I really want to know. As a Lieutenant I worked a number of overtime shifts on Rescue Four, and it was always a very entertaining area to work in.

One morning we ran on a child delivery in Rescue Four's area; it was very early. It was mom's first baby and her water had broken. She was having some contractions, but they were spaced far apart, and she was not dilated. We released the patient to the family for transport to Baptist Hospital where her doctor was waiting. We started back to the station and the paramedic in the back of the unit said, "Let's swing by Dunkin Donut and pick up some donuts for the station." I told the driver, go ahead we will probably get another call anyway before we get back to the station.

We were traveling south on US 1 Highway at about 158th Street southwest when a small pickup truck came speeding out of a parking lot on the opposite side of the highway. There had been a light rain earlier that morning and the road was wet and slick. The pickup came across the highway right in front of us. My driver did an excellent job of missing the out-of-control truck by braking and swerving to the left as the small truck passed in front of us. The small pickup then hit the gas and spun out of control in front of us crossing back across both lanes and ended up broad side right in front of us. My driver did the best job he could to stop, but on a wet street that was next to impossible. He did manage to reduce our speed considerably before we nailed the pickup broad side knocking him fifty feet sideways. The only thing that kept us from killing the driver was the wet street, nobody was getting any traction, and this reduced the impact. Our crew member in the back of the unit was buried under equipment and bandages.

The driver and I dug her out quickly to make sure she was OK. She was bruised but OK. As we climbed out of the back of the rescue to check out the two guys in the pickup they started up the motor and proceeded to leave the scene of the accident. My driver asked what are we going to do, and I said, "Let's catch them." So we jumped in the rescue truck now sporting a large dent in the right front fender but no real tire or motor damage. I suspected this was not the case for the pickup truck.

As we chased them south on US 1, I called the alarm office, Dade County, Rescue 4, QSK (what is your message) Rescue 4? I advised we had been involved in an auto accident and were now chasing the other vehicle involved south on US 1 at a high rate of speed. As you might imagine there was a long silence on the radio. Maybe I should have left out "at a high rate of speed." Then the alarm office responded, could you repeat that? I responded, we were hit by a pickup truck that subsequently is attempting to flee the scene of the accident, and we are chasing the vehicle south on US 1. After several miles on US 1 the pickup turned west on southwest 168th Street. We are requesting police assistance in apprehending the vehicle. Reaching speeds of 70 miles per hour or so west bound on 168th Street.

I was thinking to myself about how to compose the letter to the Chief. *"Dear Chief, We were headed to the donut shop, minding our own business, when we were hit by an out of control pickup truck. Then we chased him after he left the scene at high speed through the southwest section of Dade County with your fire rescue truck."*

About that time the pickup truck started smoking and oil and fluids could be seen coming from the engine compartment. I told my driver this chase is about over. The driver asked what to I do if they jump out with a gun? I said, "Run over them."

He paused for a minute and then said, "OK."

Finally, just before reaching Krome Avenue the pickup truck ground to a halt. We had our spotlights trained on the vehicle so we could see them a lot better than they could see us. I ordered both the driver and passenger to get out of the vehicle and put their hands on the roof. The passenger replied, "You can't make me do that, you are not a cop. Noting that the soon to be victim was somewhat smaller than me and not nearly as mad, I stated, you wrecked my rescue truck, injured my crew and fled the scene of an accident with injuries. If you don't put your hands on the roof of the vehicle and keep them there, you are going to make my day. Believe me, because I am going to open up a large can of "whip ass."

Some of our weapons are primitive; like pike axes, hydrant wrenches, but they are effective. After quite some time the police arrived, they jokingly said, "What are you guys trying to do put us out of a job?"

I thought to myself, *with no tag number if we had not run them down, they would have never been caught.* When the police gave the driver a sobriety test, you know the one where you place your finger on your nose and lean back. Well, the driver fell right over backwards; it was amazing he could drive at all. We never did get to pick up the donuts it was after shift change before we got back to the station, and I still had to write a letter to the Chief and fill out an accident report.

Chapter Nine
FROM RIOTS IN WATTS, CALIFORNIA TO RIOTS IN MIAMI IN 1968

Miami from 1968 until the 1980s was the testing grounds for police and firemen. We had nine riots during these trying times. The rioters were angry and not satisfied with the way they were treated. Oftentimes I believe they were whipped up by radical members from out of town. One incident involving alleged police brutality was all it would take to spark a riot. The young militant and radical rioters took to the street shooting and killing a number of people and burning millions of dollars' worth of property to the ground. Many of the businesses that were burned were stores that had extended credit to young mothers who had no money to buy food for their children. In just one of the riots nineteen innocent people were killed, and 100 million dollars' worth of property was destroyed. Thanks to the efforts of community leaders, most of the potential riots were diffused in later years.

Believe me it was not pleasant fighting fires with people shooting at you and throwing Molotov cocktails at the fire trucks in route to fires. Each unit had a police escort, two cars with six heavily armed officers in each car. One in front of the fire engine and one in the back. We pulled close to the buildings on fires and used 3-inch jump lines with large nozzles to extinguish fires. We had to leave the area to refill our tank (500 to 1000 gallons depending on the unit). All too often the fires rekindled or were reignited before we returned. We could not lay lines to fight the fires because this would draw a crowd and was not safe. Miami's problems followed the riots in Watts in California by about two years. If you want to know what is going to happen in Miami watch California, it will happen in Miami two years later. I am very glad those issues were resolved now all Miami has to deal with is road rage and crime.

Chapter Ten
THE REDLANDS 1975

S outh Dade County is a rural farming area with lots of residential homes and businesses. The area known as the "Redlands" is famous for high speed deceleration accidents. Lots of large farm equipment and trucks frequent these roads and when a regular size auto tangles with a large truck the result is not pretty. I had begun building a home in the Florida Keys just twenty miles from Key West, when I transferred to the Redlands in 1975. I planned on commuting from Cudjoe Key in the Lower Keys to the fire station in the Redlands for about the next twenty years. The drive was not that bad, considering I would be driving up in the early morning hours when traffic was light. It was a two- and half-hour drive, and I would arrive at the fire station at 6:00 a.m. for my 7:00 a.m. shift. Our shift is 24-hours long and we get off at 7:00 a.m. the next day. Then we are off for 48 hours. In an effort to reduce our working hours we were given a Croy Day. This day was named after Chief Croy who came up with the idea. If your Croy Day was on a Wednesday, you would be off on that shift. That gave us five days off in a row.

During the next eighteen years I would become thoroughly familiar with US Highway 1 from Cudjoe Key to South Miami. Most of that time I drove over the old bridges in the Florida Keys; they were very narrow. The road was laid on top of the old railroad bridges with barely enough room for two cars to pass. There were no radio stations on the air that early in the morning, so I had a tape deck, lots of coffee and a CB radio to keep me awake.

The CB radio was very entertaining and allowed me to get to know a lot of people

I would never have met. All the truckers had CB radios and chatting back and forth became a pass-time. There were also a lot of base stations along the way in houses and even the bridge tenders had CB radios. My handle was the "Conch Train." It wasn't long before I knew most of them, and they knew me. The bridge tender on the channel two bridge would call me to see where I was, when a boat would need the bridge opened. She would say, you better speed it up honey if you want make the bridge, and she would hold off if she could until I passed.

One morning on my way up to the fire station I got a call on the CB from an old friend, he asked me if I could swing by one of the docks in Key Largo and help out a friend of his. He reassured me it was on the up and up. I stopped by the dock. Now this is five o'clock in the morning, mind you. When I got out of my truck, I saw a young man sitting in his car. I walked over and he said would you mind tying my rod and reel on the stern of this drift boat. Apparently if you place your rod in that spot, you have reserved it for the day's fishing. I could see that he was a paraplegic, so I tied the rod in his spot and we got into a conversation. He said the captain of the boat would not let him fish on the side of the boat. I asked why not. Well, he said it was rough one day and the brakes on my wheelchair failed and I mowed down about ten fishermen before I got stopped. There was quite an angle (downward slope on the side of the boat). Whenever he would call me, I would stop by and place his rod on the stern. One of our rescues had pulled him out of a bad auto accident several years previously.

Another gentleman I got to know lived up in Key Largo, his CB handle was Winkey. I don't remember his name. He was in his late seventies and had lost his eyesight. We talked many times on the CB and I would stop by his house on occasion if he needed something. He told me that his father was the engineer on the train from Homestead to Key West when he was a boy. The railroad that whet to sea literally. He related stories from his youth when he would ride the train down to the seven-mile bridge where his father would drop him off, and then he would fish until the train returned, and he would ride back to Key Largo. He had some really big fish stories about sharks and Jew fish that lived under the bridge. The time frame we are talking about here is in the 1920s. The railroad was washed out to sea in the 1935 Hurricane.

I stopped to help out rescue workers on auto accidents in the Keys on the way to work many times. Sometimes I would jump in the rescue and ride with them to the hospital to help stabilize patients. I was skilled in starting IVs using air way devices and other equipment they carried but were not yet trained to use. My Captain, Dave Frame always held over the off-going crew until I could get there, when he knew I was involved in a rescue effort.

My First Shift at Station Five

I WILL NEVER FORGET my first shift at Metro Dade Fire Station Five. Station Five is located on Hobson Drive just off US 1 about southwest 238th Street in the

Redlands. Our territory was one of the largest in the department covering all of the southern part of the county including the eighteen mile stretch, the Card Sound Road and the road to Flamingo. The eighteen-mile stretch is a deadly stretch of US Highway 1, linking Homestead and Key Largo in the Florida Keys. The Card Sound Road is a very dangerous narrow road from Homestead to Ocean Reef in Key Largo. The highway from Florida City to Flamingo, some 60 miles, was also in our territory not to mention miles of country roads winding through the farmlands of the Redlands. When I arrived at Station Five on my first shift I, was introduced to the crews and D. L. Causey was the tanker driver. With limited supply of fire hydrants, the tanker was our water supply carrying 5000 gallons of water. Sonny Kapple was our engine driver, the engine carried 1000 gallons of water for the same reason. Our Battalion Commander was Captain Dave Frame a no nonsense kind of guy and a great boss to work for. I was the Lieutenant on the rescue and my crew was made up of my driver Jerry Reed ex Air Force Ranger who had been assigned to protect the president of the United States and a great joke teller, and Nino Spadaro. Nino was a great guy, a good paramedic and easy to work with; he always carried more than his share of the load.

I arrived early that first morning and was greeted by D.L., a very large intimidating man with a heart about the size of a refrigerator. I had been warned about D.L., he was a great jokester. I got a cup of coffee and sat down in the small kitchen. D.L., a firefighter, walked over and put a dish towel over the top of my head. "Sorry, Lieutenant," he said, "the glare was blinding me. Since the age of 21 I didn't have any hair on the top of my head." From this point on I knew we were going to get along fine.

At about three o'clock in the afternoon on that first shift we receive a report of a truck/car accident on southwest 232nd Street and 192nd Avenue. Knowing it was my first day in unfamiliar territory, Capt. Frame assigned himself and an additional engine company for manpower. When we arrived on the scene, we discovered a van had run a stop street, colliding with a farm truck. The driver of the truck was OK but the people inside the van were badly injured. All three of the Spadaro brothers were on the scene within minutes. They lived close by and heard the crash. One young boy had an arm all but torn off and was bleeding uncontrollably. As luck would have it a police helicopter landed on the scene, and we put Niño on the side of the chopper holding the boy and they flew him to Homestead Hospital only minutes away by air. Of the five people in the van, two adults and three children, only two survived. The helicopter ride saved the boy's life.

Later back at the station, D.L. said, "Welcome to the Redlands."

I had seen lots of trauma in my career but the Redlands over the next twenty years would redefine high-speed deceleration trauma. Overloaded vans involved in high-speed accidents were actually common in the Redlands. In a rural area like the Redlands the

30

speed limit is 55 miles per hour unless otherwise posted. The passengers were usually not belted in and sat on the same buckets they would pick the vegetables with. I remember one van accident where the van collided with a big truck. The van was carrying 22 farm workers, and no one was belted in. Twenty-two critically injured patients in the middle of rural south Dade, miles from medical help, is a real challenge. Although there were a number of Chiefs on this scene I was given a free hand to call all the shots. I had handled more of these type of calls than I care to remember, and my superiors were well aware of my rescue, extrication and triage skills.

The first order of business is to assign paramedics to injuries that are immediately life threatening. I sized up the number of patients and their medical needs. I asked the alarm office to dispatch the two closest rescue units to assist the two rescues, two engines and ladder truck I had on scene. Then I requested six additional medical rescue trucks to assist in transporting the victims to hospitals. Our rescue helicopters were still several years away, boy we sure could have used them on this call. We set up a triage center 200 feet away from the accident scene where victims were still trapped in the wreckage and the "jaws of life" were being used to free them.

The "jaws of life" are a set of hydraulically operated jaws, resembling a very large set of scissors. The hydraulic pump is operated by a small air-cooled motor and a series of hydraulic lines extend to the jaws. The tip of the jaws can exert 50,000 pounds of pressure. They can literally rip a car door open in seconds. The air-cooled motor is noisy and can make communications difficult. It is important to distance workers and patients from the noise and confusion so we could work and communicate. Our rescue crews worked feverishly to establish air ways, control bleeding, establish IV lines, splint broken bones, while the engine and ladder crews worked to free trapped victims with the "jaws of life." Three trauma levels of patients were established for transport at the triage area, according to the most serious of injuries. Before victims could be transported, I had to communicate with the receiving hospitals, the patient's needs and confirm the number of patients each hospital could handle. The nearest trauma center was Jackson Memorial Hospital some twenty-five miles away. Homestead Hospital, Coral Reef Hospital and Baptist Hospital were closer. As the additional rescue units began to arrive, patients were transported to area hospitals according to their needs and the hospitals ability to accept them. A few years down the road with the arrival of our medical rescue transport helicopters, this type of call would have been much simpler, and the patients would have gone directly to trauma units.

Rescue Units Have Run-in with Highway Patrol

MOST OF THE TIME fire and rescue work very closely with the police and have a good relationship, but not always. There was a short time in south end of Dade County when the Rescues and the Highway Patrol had some serious issues over patient treatment and transport. Several Florida Highway Patrolmen (FHP) in the late 1970s decided they were in charge of the scene and would dictate to the Dade County Rescue were they would transport patients. These FHP officers got tired of having to drive to a distant hospital to finish their report when there was a closer hospital, and they would not have to drive as far. The officers began ordering the Rescues to transport to the closest hospital. Several of our units did not feel it was important enough to go up against the FHP and make an issue of it.

Well once again I always end up in the wrong place at the right time. We had a rescue on a driver that began having heart palpitations while driving and pulled over and called 911. I was riding Rescue Six at the time and responded to the call. Upon examination, the patient displayed runs of ventricular tachycardia the patient's history revealed he had a pacemaker inserted several years before and it was apparently not responding to the arrhythmia. This can lead to ventricular fibrillation or cardiac arrest. The closest hospital was James Archer Smith in Homestead. However, the patient's doctor was waiting at Coral Reef Hospital, and Coral Reef had the equipment to treat the patient's problem and James Archer did not. The FHP arrived on the scene, and I noted that the officer was one of the officers that ordered rescues to transport to the closest hospital. We had started a IV and were preparing to transport to Coral Reef. The FHP officer stated he would meet us at Homestead, and I responded we are transporting to Coral Reef. He immediately responded I am in charge of the scene, and you will transport to Homestead. I informed him that I was charged with the medical responsibility of the patient, and it is not in his best interest.

I stepped out of the rescue unit because I did not want to alarm the patient knowing this was going to get unpleasant. The FHP officer stated you will transport to Homestead, or I will arrest you. I informed my rescue crew to prepare to transport to Coral Reef and held out my hands so the officer could handcuff me. The officer said, "Put your hands down." I then stepped into the street and held my hands up and began walking toward the police car. Traffic began stopping to look at the scene. I informed the officer that in five minutes I was transporting to Coral Reef, and he better arrest me or get out of the way. The officer stated I can arrest you for refusing a police order. I countered I can have you arrested for interfering with a fire officer in the performance of his duty. I further informed the officer; you better be good at letter writing if that patient dies in the back of my truck while you are arresting me. The officer seemed confused as to what to do so I climbed in the rescue, and we transported to Coral Reef where the patient's doctor was waiting. Later the FHP officer came to Coral Reef and the head nurse cussed him out and physically threw him out of the emergency room.

On arrival back at the station the phone was ringing off the hook. The next day we had a big meeting with FHP and Fire officials and resolved the problem. Needless to say the Fire Department made the medical decisions and it was some time before the rescue crew spoke to the FHP officers involved. Most of the time we got along very well.

Chapter Eleven
ARRIVAL OF AIR RESCUE
TRANSPORT HELICOPTERS

The arrival of the medical transport helicopters was one of the biggest improvements in the rescue service particularly in rural areas. In trauma injuries, not unlike cardiac emergencies, time is a very important factor. Over sixty percent of patients with cardiac emergencies die in the first two hours. Treatment of arrhythmias and administering clot busting medication is pivotal to the patient's long-term survival. "Time is Muscle" lose the heart muscle or fail to treat the arrhythmia, and you lose the patient. In trauma injuries you must respect the "Golden Hour." A trauma patient must reach a trauma center within the first hour after the accident. If surgeons are going to have a fighting chance to save their lives they must get in there to fix the damage before vital organs begin shutting down.

Transporting to trauma centers with helicopters brought a new level of excitement to rescues. In a busy intersection two cars collided, one of the victims was not wearing a seat belt. His car hit the other car then his body flew forward colliding with the dash and steering wheel, then the third collision his internal organs flew forward colliding with his skeletal structure, resulting in a lacerated spleen and liver. Rescue is dispatched and upon arrival call for helicopter transport to a level one trauma center Jackson Memorial Hospital.

Two engine companies are dispatched and block the roadway on either side of the accident so the Bell 412 twin-jet helicopter can land to pick up the trauma patient. The helicopter lands and the patient is loaded in the helicopter, two paramedics from the on-scene rescue unit board the air rescue unit to treat the victim while in flight. Six minutes later the helicopter lands on the roof of the Jackson Trauma Center and the patient is rushed into the operating room.

From the time of the accident, thirty-six minutes have passed, and the patient will do fine, still in that "Golden Hour." When I was stationed in Homestead at Station 16, we responded to quite a number of gunshot victims. One shooting occurred just outside the fire house. Soon as the shooter was gone and the police were on the scene, we responded. We positioned the rescue truck right next to the gunshot victim, pulled the stretcher out of the truck and loaded the patient. The victim was shot in the upper right chest with a large-bore gun. The victim was barely conscious with a BP of 60 over 40 and a 120 pulse. We started two IVs one in each arm with 18- gauge catheters and ringer's lactate. The Mast suit was inflated. The victim was also treated for a sucking chest wound using Vaseline gauze. The Air Rescue Helicopter was close by and was on the scene in minutes. We loaded the victim and flew him to Jackson Trauma Center. The patient was in the Trauma unit in nineteen minutes from the time the call came in. Possibly the only downside to this is with the patient's rapid and full recovery the rematch may occur the next weekend.

Chapter Twelve
THE LAWSUIT

To our knowledge no firefighters had ever been sued in a civil lawsuit, prior to 1980, but then I always seemed to be on the leading edge of things strange and bazaar. It was just after dark on a Sunday evening when a family of Mexican migrant farm workers decided to drive from the labor camp located on southwest 137 Avenue and 312nd Street to the Homestead Armory where a dance was being held. The driver of this 1973 Chevy Suburban was many times legally drunk when his blood was tested twenty-four hours after the accident. Twelve other members of the family and several friends climbed into the Suburban for the drive to the Homestead Armory approximately four miles away. Three of the thirteen people in the suburban were age 33 to 50 years of age, the other ten were children ages 2 to 16.

They drove along 312th Street headed west toward Homestead, a two-lane rural road with a small drainage ditch on the north side of the roadway. This drainage ditch was just a little wider than a car and had about three to four feet of water in it. The drainage ditch was shrouded by weeds and beyond the ditch to the north was a potato field.

As the highly intoxicated driver drove west on 312nd Street, he began to stray across the center line headed into oncoming traffic. An oncoming car flashed his high beams to warn the driver. The driver of the Suburban over-corrected crossing back over the center line, across his lane, down the shoulder of the road and impacted the north wall of the drainage ditch at about a 45-degree angle. A trial of hash marks 132 feet in length marked the path of the vehicle as it careened toward the ditch. These hash marks would later prove invaluable in the defense of the lawsuit.

When the suburban impacted the north limestone wall of the drainage ditch, one passenger, (Bertha Lopez) a 50-year-old female, was ejected through the front windshield landing about twenty feet to the north of the impact area in a potato field. After the initial impact with the north wall of the ditch, the Suburban most likely tumbled end over end landing on its roof in the ditch 30 to 40 feet west of the impact area. Substantial damage was noted on the front and rear of the vehicle. Twelve people were now trapped inside the upside-down vehicle in black darkness with water rushing in. Lucky for some in the vehicle the water was not deep enough to fully flood the car. There was about eighteen inches of air space at the floor (top) between the seats.

The vehicle was now divided into compartments with the seats separating the areas inside. The crushed rear end of the vehicle was stacked with baby strollers and other equipment. The ditch was only inches wider than the car so doors could not be opened even if they were not jammed by the impact. The front of the car was completely crushed leaving no escape route. Word spread quickly to the nearby Mexican labor camp at 139th Avenue and southwest 312th Street and many of the Mexicans rushed to the scene. We found out later there was perhaps as much as a 35-minute delay in the initial report of the accident to fire and police. The Mexican people prefer to handle things on their own not involving outsiders. It was obvious when we arrived on the scene that large pry bars had been used to try and open the doors of the vehicle, several were left on the scene. They were trying to free those trapped inside the vehicle, and perhaps knowing that the driver was very intoxicated, they wanted to get him out before the police arrived. In a number of accidents occurring in this area with migrants involved, if they could move the migrants would flee the scene of the accident before fire and police arrived.

Chapter Thirteen
THE RESCUE

At 8:33 p.m. Sunday on January 13, 1980, Rescue 6 received a call from the Dade County Alarm Office of a car in the canal at approximately 139th Avenue and 312th Street southwest. Responding from Station 6 at southwest 288th Street and Old Dixie Highway I requested the alarm office to dispatch Rescue 16, Engine 16 and Ladder 16 from Station 16 in Homestead, Engine 6 was already in route. Metro Dade Police were also responding. Having a great deal of experience in these type of accidents in the Redlands, I knew this call could involve large numbers of accident victims, and this close to the Labor Camp we would need crowd control on the scene. On previous calls in this area intoxicated crowds required police presence for control of the scene. At 8:39, Rescue 6 arrived on scene, several police units and approximately 25 to 30 migrant workers were on the scene.

After being briefed by the police officers who arrived first on the scene I informed the police commander that I was assuming command of the Rescue. My initial assessment of the scene was that this was going to be a really tough rescue, requiring extrication through an opening made with the "jaws of life." The vehicle obviously had high-speed impacts in the front and rear of the Suburban. This indicated there would be multiple high-speed deceleration injuries in the accident victims. The vehicle was upside down on its roof in a ditch no wider than the vehicle. This is a rural area, miles from hospitals. I was able to check the vehicle for stability, it was secure lying on the solid rock bottom of the ditch. In my initial briefing by the police, they reported seeing several Mexican migrants standing on the vehicle trying to free the victims with pry bars.

I could hear the people inside the vehicle but could not see them. I reassured them that lots of help was on the way, and we would get them out very quickly. My driver and paramedic Mike Simpson discovered the victim lying in the field (Bertha Lopez) twenty feet north of the ditch were the Suburban initial impact was. Mike began an examination of Bertha to determine her medical status and injuries. Bertha was apparently ejected through the front windshield on the initial impact with the north wall of the ditch. With obvious head injuries and a fractured femur and most likely internal injuries she was immobilized on a backboard and ringer IV started. Although her vitals were stable, femur fractures can pool a lot of blood in the leg and these patients can go into shock very quickly.

I contacted the alarm office to double check, one that the extra units were on the way, and that the "jaws of life" were on the units and two I had the alarm office begin a check of the hospitals in the area to determine how many patients each could handle. The alarm office confirmed that the units were on the way and two sets of "jaws of life" were in fact on the units. In this type of rescue the "jaws of life" are the only way to open crushed metal doors to gain excess to the passenger compartments. I remember the old days when the jaws of life were 45-minutes to an hour away, only one set in the south end. The only other jaws were on Air Force Rescue One that responded with us many times from the Air Force Base. Now thanks to the taxpayers of Metro Dade County most of our rescues, engines, and ladder trucks carried the "jaws."

I asked the police if they could set up a safety zone around the scene to keep on lookers from getting hurt or getting in our way. The police were expecting more units to arrive in minutes including Homestead Police and the Highway Patrol. Containing this crowd was going to be a big problem due to intoxication and the fact friends and family were in the car and emotions were running high. Rescue 16 was the first unit to arrive on the scene with the jaws. I took a minute to brief Lieutenant Ron Easely on the situation and my observations. There was a small area on the far side of the ditch where the side of the ditch was eroded away leaving just a few inches of room to use the jaws to force open the back door and gain excess to the vehicle. The migrants had started a small hole where the jaws could begin tearing the metal apart. This was at the bottom of the door remembering the vehicle is upside down lying on its roof and the windows are down. My plan was to open up this area first and get a rescue man inside to begin evaluation and extrication of the victims in that compartment.

The vehicle is now divided into three, possibly four, compartments separated by the seats and water. Only eighteen inches of air is at the top of the compartments. The rest of the car is flooded with water from the ditch. The jaws crushed open the door wide enough to get our first rescue man inside the vehicle. While Bill Broughton was evaluating the patients in that compartment, I directed the team operating the jaws to begin opening the front door by crushing the metal to the side in a similar manner to create an opening. I

38

designated an area on the roadway to be the triage area and men and backboards were standing by to transport the injured to the area after initial splinting of obvious fractures and stabilizing necks, etc. Just fifteen minutes after Rescue 6 arrived on the scene and took command, the first victim was extricated from the vehicle and carried to the triage area. Bertha Lopez was already in the triage area, she did not have to be extricated, she was ejected on the first impact.

Ladder 16 and Engine 6 had set up their portable generators to provide plenty of light for the rescue workers at the overturned vehicle and the triage area. One of the problems was that the intoxicated and grief-stricken migrants kept walking through the area blocking light and stepping on patients and equipment. The police were walking a tight line between crowd control and a riot, doing the best job they could under the circumstances. One by one the victims were removed from the overturned vehicle compartment by compartment, nine serious to critical trauma patients were removed. There were thirteen victims in the vehicle at the time of the accident, one ejected through the front windshield and twelve trapped in the car.

After all the live patients were extricated, paramedics in the vehicle asked me if I wanted the D.O.A. (dead on arrival) removed. I asked them to hold off until the scene was more secure. Our main responsibility now was to treat the injured and get them to the best hospital facility that could treat their injuries. Bringing out three dead children at this point would have turned the scene into a nightmare, more so than it was already.

The scene became more secure as additional police officers arrived and moved the crowd out of the triage area. Paramedics were able to work and transport units could be brought to the scene and patients loaded for transport to local hospitals. After the injured were removed from the scene, the crowd dispersed and calmed down. We then began the grim task of removing the dead, most of which were children. This was very hard on many of the firefighters because they had children of their own about the same age.

Suddenly one of the Mexican laborers came running through the security area jumping from the roadway onto the back of Lt. Pete Hendricks. Hendricks fell to the ground but still maintained a hold on the backboard containing one of the deceased children. The man was very emotional, completely overcome by the scene. Several police officers escorted the man from the immediate scene, he then sat voluntarily in the back of one of the police cars trying to regain his composure. This was not the first-time members of the crowd jumped upon the rescuers' backs in sheer frustration.

The driver of the vehicle was not found. The question was raised could he be trapped under the vehicle or did he leave the scene? Leaving the scene of an accident with fatalities is a felony. Two Metro Dade Police units were dispatched to the driver's house in the nearby Mexican Labor Camp. In unit one officers Gordon Gouwens and Theron McClain responded to the driver of the vehicle's home address, unit number 208 in the Mexican labor camp located at 137th Avenue and 312nd Street southwest. Officers Kevin Long and Gordon Gouwens backed up unit one. When they arrived at the address Gouwens and McClain knocked on the front door and Kevin Long and Allan Holley positioned themselves at the back door. No one was home at the address, the officers then discovered that the numbering system in the camp had recently been changed. They were directed to a second address by a relative. At the second address they spoke with an aunt, and she informed them that Juan Suarez, the driver, was not home. The Officers asked the aunt to have Juan call the police if he did return home. The officers then returned to the scene of the accident. Detective Thomas Burns of the Traffic Investigations Unit had arrived on the scene and began his investigation. Detective Burns requested that Dr. Charles V. Wetli, the Dade County Medical Examiner, respond to the scene. Dr. Wetli and Detective Burns examined the three female victims at the scene. The location of the driver of the vehicle was still not known. A more extensive examination of the victims would be conducted at the Medical Examiner's Office. After Dr. Wetli departed the scene, Detective Burns had the tow truck driver remove the car from the canal. The driver's location was no longer a mystery when the vehicle was removed from the canal. The driver was found pinned under the front dash of the auto trapped in twisted metal.

Chapter Fourteen
AUTOPSIES DETERMINE
THE CAUSE OF DEATH

On Monday January 14, 1980, Dr. Wetli performed autopsies on the four victims, which revealed the individual causes of death as:

Victim # 1
Juan Suarez, White/Male/40 years of age
Cause of death: Drowning with a contributing cause of death listed as Acute Ethanolism
The driver was drunk with a blood alcohol level of .150 percent

Victim # 2
Maria Suarez, white/female/7 years of age: Fracture of the neck

Victim # 3
Nora Lopez, white/female/age 3: Drowning

Victim # 4
Blanca Martinez, white/female/19: Drowning

Arturo Gomez had the grim task of identifying the victims at the Medical Examiner's Office. After examining the bodies, Dr. Charles Wetli concluded the following:
   a. Juan Suarez - Mr. Suarez was intoxicated and death was due to drowning. He stated that he probably expired within 2-3 minutes after impact.
   b. Maria Suarez –had a broken neck and died instantly.
   c. Blanca Martinez – death was due to drowning. She had two broken ribs, a punctured left lung, and a severely ruptured spleen. Both the left lung and spleen were bleeding profusely. A large quantity of blood was lost. Dr. Wetli stated that she could not have survived more than 5-6 minutes without medical assistance.
   d. Nora Lopez – Death was due to drowning. She sustained a contusion to her head and was possibly unconscious and drowned within 2-3 minutes.

Dr. Wetli was apprised of the estimated time of the accident and the time of arrival for the first police officers on the scene. It is his opinion that all four of the victims were either dead or agonal by the time the first officer arrived on the scene.

Items recovered by the Metro Dade Police Dive Team included a white vinyl purse and its contents. The contents included two twenty-dollar bills, one ten-dollar bill, one dollar and sixty-four cents, one yellow in color ring with clear stone. Total currency $51.64. Also recovered from the scene was a pair of leather boots.

The driver of the vehicle, Juan Suarez, had on his person; One brown leather like wallet and personal papers and contents, one nail clipper, one Caravel wristwatch with black strap, one plastic comb. The wallet contained five twenty-dollar bills, thirty-one ten-dollar bills, ten five-dollar bills and five one-dollar bills all U.S. currency. A total of $465.00. These items were discovered by detective T.M. Burns of the Metro Dade Police Department.

Chapter Fifteen
ALLEGATIONS BEGIN TO SURFACE

On January 16, 1980, Major E. Gonzalez, South Regional Commander of the Metro Dade Police Department attended a meeting at the St. Ann's Church, 13890 southweest 264th Street Miami, Florida. The meeting was held by friends and family members of people involved in a traffic accident which occurred on January 13, 1980, at southwest 312th Street approximately one mile west of 137th Avenue. Several complaints were made at the meeting concerning the manner in which P.S.D. (Public Safety Department) and Fire Rescue personnel handled the situation. Major Gonzalez requested that the Internal Review initiate an investigation, regarding the complaints on January 17, 1980.

On January 18, 1980, another meeting was held regarding the incident by the Latin American League Against Discrimination (LALAD). The meeting was held at the community center, 970 S. W. 1st Street Miami, Florida. This investigator (Major Gonzales) attended the meeting and listened to the complaints registered by friends and family members.

Mr. Jose Hernandez was one of the more outspoken family members in attendance. Mr. Hernandez's complaints were as follows:

1. That he, along with other friends and relatives, was not permitted to conduct his own rescue attempts.

2. That the police just stood around for approximately fifteen minutes without taking any action to affect the rescue.
3. That the police did not communicate with family members in the crowd as to what actions they had taken.
4. That the police had threatened them and pushed them around.

Alfredo Hernandez, son of Jose Hernandez, was one of the victims trapped in the submerged vehicle. He complained that the weight of the police and fire rescue personnel walking on top of the vehicle caused the vehicle to sink deeper into the canal thus increasing the risk of their drowning. He also complained of gasoline leaking from the gas tank into the canal. He complained that the leak may have been caused by police and fire personnel walking on the gasoline tank.

Mrs. Magaly Sanchez, a spokesperson for the group, complained that approximately $1200 cash and two purses are unaccounted for. She stated that the driver of the vehicle, Juan Suarez, was carrying approximately $1000 cash.

Benito Carlos, State Director of the Migrant Association complained that officers broke into the home of Juan Suarez and searched for him. He stated that during the entry they pushed Eliazar Lopez aside and they had their weapons drawn.

A complaint was also made that one of the crowd members, Hector Martinez, had his shirt torn off by P.S.D.

Guillermo Gonzales also complained that he was not permitted to conduct rescue efforts.

A similar meeting was also held by the Chief of the Metro Dade Fire Department, Edward Donaldson. Chief Donaldson tried to make peace with the migrants' family and friends but learned a tough lesson when the migrants twisted his words to satisfy themselves. Then the newspapers can report what the migrants say to make shocking headlines. This is how the newspapers sell newspapers and reporting what the migrants say doesn't have to be true. The newspaper, in other words, can tell lies with no legal responsibility, because the migrants said it, not the *Miami Herald*. Chief Donaldson, in an effort to reach some middle ground with the unreasonable group stated, "perhaps the fire rescue person used poor judgment." Headlines in the *Miami Herald* read "Fire Chief Ed Donaldson states firemen used poor judgment." The Fire Department has had little or no experience dealing with complaints, firemen had always been the good guys.

The police on the other hand right or wrong are always being attacked by some person or group. This was a first for Donaldson, he quickly found out why the Police department has an internal review board. They are accustomed to accusations and complaints. The review boards gather the information, review the information, gather statements from the officers involved and then make a determination. In short, gather the data and keep your mouth shut, so they don't stick your foot in your mouth.

This was just the beginning of a number of false accusations by LALAD, and the migrant workers' family and friends made to local newspapers. Other headlines read

"Police and Fire Hand Out Matches and Cigars with Gasoline in the Ditch." Another read: "Firemen Play Catch with a Dead Baby While Family Members Drown in the Vehicle. There were about ten or twelve similar headline articles in the several different newspapers including the *Miami Herald* and *Fort Lauderdale Sentinel*, *Homestead-Florida City News* and others.

I personally could not believe a newspaper would print such false information. I called our P.R. representative Stu Kauffman and told him I will own the *Miami Herald* for printing such lies. Stu took me aside and said, "Let me tell you how this works. A newspaper can take what you say and what Jose Rodriguez says and print it and they have no legal responsibility. When the newspaper starts editorializing, they are legally responsible for what they say and they better be correct."

I stopped to reflect on the moment. *You know it is strange to me that a family puts twelve members of their family and friends into a vehicle with a driver that is more than three times legally drunk, no safety belts, not enough seats for the passengers, then crashes the overloaded vehicle into a stone wall of a ditch exceeding the speed limit, and then blames the fire and police for the accident.*

Chapter Sixteen
CIVILIANS ARE INTOXICATED AND UNRULY

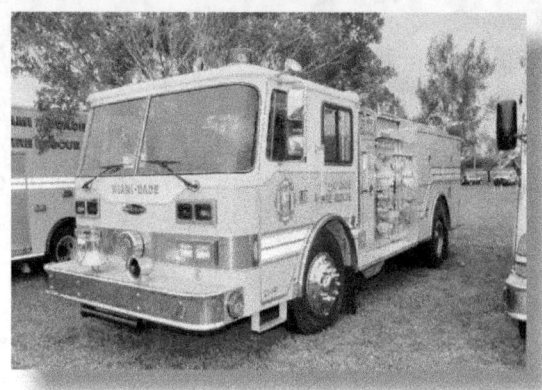

Civilians on the scene (non-migrant laborers and sober) stated in an interview that there was a crowd of more than 100 migrant workers and many were intoxicated and unruly.

Richard Bush gave a verbal statement; he was dispatched to the scene to provide wrecker service. Mr. Bush stated he did not see the metro police strike or threaten anyone, and that the crowd was unruly and smoking despite repeated request by the police not to smoke. Mr. Bush stated that it took two wreckers to remove the vehicle, partly due to the way it was wedged between the two walls of the ditch. He stated that when he walked on the vehicle it did not sink or move at all.

Sgt. Peter Christolini, Homestead Police, stated when he arrived at the scene all live victims had been removed from the car and were being treated. He states that it was obvious that some of the crowd had been drinking. He estimated the crowd to be approximately 200 people.

Highway Patrol officer G.P. "Bucky" Buchanan gave a verbal statement. He stated that he was requested to the scene by Highway Patrol Officer Bostick—reference unruly spectators. He stated that when he arrived at the scene three Mexican males were attempting to push past the roadblock set up just west of the scene. The Mexican males were intoxicated and refusing to stop. He stated they were turned away. One of the three subjects a few minutes later jumped on top on the accident vehicle and had to be removed.

After investigators interviewed hundreds of people on the scene, they determined that the Police and Fire Rescue personnel had conducted themselves in a highly professional manner and had saved the lives of those victims that were not killed on the initial high-speed impact with the walls of the ditch. It was further determined that the crowd was highly emotional due to the fact family and friends were involved, and many were intoxicated and unruly.

Chapter Seventeen
THE CIVIL LAWSUIT IS FILED

After accident and subsequent investigations into the actions of Fire and Police showed there was no negligence on their part. But a fellow by the name of Benito Carlos kept fanning the flames. Carlos, the Migrant Associations Director, in the *Homestead Newspaper* claimed the Metro Police stood by and watched as four people drowned in an overturned vehicle that Saturday night. Carlos said, "The people are dissatisfied with the treatment. Tension is running high."

Lopez also stated that more than twenty fire and police officers ignored the screams and the pleas of the people struggling inside the auto, the newspaper reported. He stated that the families of the deceased farm workers needed money to pay for the burial and hospital bills for those critically injured.

The local newspapers were very unkind to the police and fire fighters, using the jaded lies of Carlos to sell newspapers. The newspapers were very careful not to editorialize these statements, because they knew they would be sued. All this trashing about in the headlines was bound to draw attention from "Sharks" just as an injured fish floundering in the surf. The first Shark Attack came from attorney Robert Williamson. Now what brings a fancy Coral Gables attorney to Homestead sniffing around in a drainage ditch.

I will let you draw your own conclusions on that one. Injustice perhaps?

A few months later a Civil Lawsuit was filed in the Circuit Court of the Eleventh Judicial Circuit of Florida, in and for Dade County. Berta Lopez, as Personal

Representative of the Nora Lopez. Case number 81-16597 CA 16 This was the first of four wrongful death suits filed on behalf of the deceased victims in the accident.

It is important to note here that these lawsuits could be filed because the "Good Samaritan Act" had not been passed. The "Good Samaritan Act" was passed on February 1, 1980, only two weeks after this accident occurred. After the Good Samaritan Act was passed, in order to sue a person in an accident similar to this one, you must first prove negligence.

The four wrongful death suits were filed against James E. Sharpe and Michael Simpson (firefighters), Frank Cavalieri, Kevin Long, Gordon Gouwens and Theron McClain (police officers), Dade County, the landowner, the person who dug the drainage ditch and the State Road Department that installed the guard rail. We use this technique in fishing; it is called throwing a cast net and see what you catch.

Firefighter Simpson and I were contacted by County Attorney Addison Meyers to set up a meeting to begin the process of gathering all the information and facts important to a defense in the suit. It seemed strange to me that after all we had been through prior to the suit proving that all the accusations were false, we would now have to prove all over again that we acted in a professional manner in the best interest of our patients. In our first meeting with Addison "Sonny" Meyers, I was immediately impressed. Somehow, I thought a County Attorney would not have the presence and knowledge of a polished Coral Gables Attorney. Well in the next five years I was going to learn a lot about the courtroom, attorneys, jurors and judges-- "more than I ever wanted to know." Although not a big guy, Sonny had a certain air of confidence about him. I would later learn in the courtroom he was a collegiate wrestler.

At our first meeting, Sonny directed us toward gathering information and facts about the accident. He encouraged us to write down the events at the scene of the accident and to develop a timeline. The timeline would begin with the dispatch of the first units Rescue 6 and would list the dispatch and arrival of all the units.

Who did what and when? We knew there was a delay in reporting the accident to authorities. Family members had made several trips to the migrant labor camp for larger pry-bars before reporting the incident. This was important because the medical examiner's report showed all of the fatalities expired between one and four minutes after the accident occurred. This would also show how efficiently the rescue workers accomplished extrication, treatment and transportation of patients to appropriate hospitals. Lt. Jim Sharpe suggested that we also use these meetings to discover any changes or improvements to our rescue procedures. Lt. Sharpe was one of the most experienced officers on the department in terms of handling large multi-unit rescues involving large numbers of critically injured patients. He also had a very impressive list of accommodations and evaluations over the years.

Chapter Eighteen
FIRE AND POLICE GET SUPPORT

In a letter to the Dade County Manager Merit Stierheim, the Chairman of the Dade County Disaster Nursing Council wrote:

> On behalf of the Dade County Disaster Nursing Council, I would like to bring
> to your attention the outstanding job Lieutenant Jim Sharpe did recently in
> the dispersal of the injured in the bus accident involving school children. His
> on-scene management avoided overloading any hospital's emergency rooms
> thereby providing immediate care to the injured. I would like to compliment
> Lieutenant Jim Sharpe on a job well done. You should be very proud to have
> him as a member of the Dade County Fire Rescue Unit.
>
> Alice K. Guterman, R.N, ED. D.

In a letter Chief C. E. Sowers wrote:

> Dear Lieutenant Sharpe,
>   I want to thank you personally for the proficient manner in which you
> handled the accident involving a van load of children on April 3, 1979.
>   Your outstanding display of expertise was evident in the way you organized
> the accident scene accomplished triage, assisted the patients, and set up
> communications with Coral Reef General and James Archer Smith Hospitals.

Your performance serves as a great source of pride to me and to the Dade County Fire and Rescue Department. Congratulations, you are indeed a valuable asset to the Emergency Medical Services division and the citizens of Dade County.
Sincerely,
C.E. Sowers, Chief
Emergency Medical Services Division

In a letter Chief A.E. O'Brien wrote:

Congratulations to Lieutenant Sharpe on the handling of a very difficult accident scene. The way Lieutenant Sharpe handled this uncommon incident speeded up the treatment that the patients needed. The total patients treated by Metro Fire Rescue was twenty-three children and one adult.

Chief A.E. O'Brien

In addition to numerous letters of accommodation Lt. Sharpe received outstanding yearly evaluations from his commanding officers.

In a meeting in the Count Attorney's Office Attorney Meyers stated, "In terms of seniority on the department in rescue you are number one.

Sonny said to me at one of the meetings, "Well if they had to pick one rescue guy to pick on, they sure made a mistake picking you."

Lt. Sharpe replied, "What do you mean?"

Sonny said, "You are number one in seniority, you taught most of the department how to use the 'jaws of life,' how to set up a triage scene, prioritize treatment and transport of patients."

Lt. Sharpe replied, "Somehow that does not make me feel all warm and fussy when all my worldly assets are on the line. I have already seen the under belly of the newspapers and their unprofessional reporting. I also took note that as a County Attorney you cannot give a gift to a judge of more than twenty-five dollars, and I also know that the group of attorneys suing me last year gave $250,000 to Judge Pesta's re-election campaign. By the way, Pesta is the judge handling our suit."

Chapter Nineteen
PRE-TRIAL PREPARATIONS

At our second meeting, that was held in the county attorney's offices in the courthouse in downtown Miami the four Police officers: Frank Cavalieri, Kevin Long, Gordon Gouwens and Theron McClain who had also been named personally in the suit, met with firefighters Mike Simpson and Lt. Jim Sharpe in attorney Meyers' office. At this meeting attorney Meyers informed us that if we wanted, we could hire our own attorney to follow along with the suit in the event the Police and Fire at any point became at odds with the county, and we could defend ourselves. Attorney Meyers stressed that we would be far better off if we were together in our defense. All parties at the meeting agreed that we would be united in our defense.

During the months preceding the trial, depositions were taken from all parties and expert witnesses were contacted to represent each side. Officer Theron McClain was going through a nasty divorce with his wife and his mother was dying of cancer. Officer Frank Cavalieri had taken a position with the Arizona Highway Patrol. Officer Cavalieri while still on the Metro Police Department was involved in a high-speed chase of a robbery suspect on the eighteen-mile stretch, when the fleeing felon ran him off the road in his police cruiser and he collided head on with a car driven by an elderly man from the Florida Keys, killing him instantly. After recovering Cavalieri accepted the job with the Arizona Highway Patrol. Firefighter Mike Simpson had taken the firefighting job after being an air traffic controller. Simpson found the job of Air Traffic Controller too stressful, so he took a job on fire rescue. Hummm. Simpson was interviewed by local newspapers a number of times right after the accident, mainly because he would talk to them, and he was accessible. Lt. Sharpe on the other hand, lived in the Florida Keys just twenty miles from Key West and commuted some three hours to the fire station from his home. Sharpe relieved the stress of riding rescue in a busy city by fishing. He owned a charter boat and fished almost every day aboard his boat named the Sea Boots.

Attorney Meyers decided that the lawsuit had gotten so large and involved that he would like to bring in one more attorney in addition to the staff in the office. This attorney's name was Ron Bernstein. Sonny was a fiery young attorney ready to fight at the drop of a hat. Ron was a little older, very patient and a stickler for detail. Together they complemented each other.

As the months passed, Lt. Sharpe was still assigned to Rescue 6 at Station 6 in south Dade County at 288th Street and South Dixie Highway. During the time of the pre-trial Lt. Sharpe responded on the families of the migrant laborers that were suing him on numerous occasions. The migrants never recognized him and unbeknown to the migrants, Sharpe had worked out an agreement with neighboring Rescue 16 to come in and relieve him on the calls. He responded to several shootings and delivered at least one baby in their family and friends.

Theron McClain had several run-ins of his own. He drove up to his house, still jointly owned by his wife and him, remember he was going through a divorce, and discovered one of the attorneys suing him was dating his wife. The attorney and his wife were looking over their perspective house for the future. Needless to say McClain had somewhat of a meltdown.

Chapter Twenty
THE DEFENSE FILES FOR A MISTRIAL

Pre-trial preparations had now stretched into many months with delays. Unknown to the group, Mike Simpson had contacted an attorney of his own, Tom Murphy, to follow along with the defense. An Attorney by the name of Smith was in the same office as Tom Andy. Just before the trial, Attorney Smith moved to the office of the prosecuting attorney, Robert Williamson. Smith had been privy to all of our preparation for the coming trial. Attorney Meyers called a meeting of the group to inform us that Simpson had been dropped from the suit by the prosecuting attorney. Attorney Smith was a large intimidating man, and in the courtroom he was referred to as the Great White Shark. Smith having been privy to all our defense when he was acting attorney for Simpson and was now on the side of the group of attorneys suing us.

Lt. Sharpe pulled Sonny aside and said, "Look these attorneys gave our judge $250,000 for his election, you gave $25, now Simpson's attorney, who is privy to all our defense, has joined their side. Is this a stacked deck or what?"

Sonny said, "I am going to file for a mistrial based on the fact they have all our defense information."

Lt. Sharpe stated for the record, "I hope it goes better than our last couple of moves."

Firefighter Simpson was at the Mistrial Meeting and you could see he was under a lot of stress. Lucky for him the police officers had to check their guns at the front desk. Simpson and his attorney came over to speak to Lt. Sharpe, I suppose to offer some reason for the betrayal of the group. A reason other than to save his own ass at the expense of his brothers. Simpson suddenly turned very pale and fell to floor in a dead faint. Simpson's attorney, Tom Andy, immediately stepped back and exclaimed, "Let Lt. Sharpe treat him; he is an expert."

Lt. Sharpe stepped back and calmly said, "Oh hell, he just fainted; he will recover in a day or two. Elevate his feet and pour some cold water on him; he will be fine."

Simpson had a long history of not doing well under pressure. I sent him in the back of an ambulance years earlier to treat a patient in route to the hospital. When I arrived at the hospital the ambulance attendant was literally shoveling emcees out of the back of the ambulance. I made the mistake of asking him what happened! He informed me that the patient (heart attack victim) threw up, then Simpson immediately threw up also.

At the mistrial meeting with Judge Pesta, Attorney Meyers and Bernstein presented the evidence and called for a mistrial. Judge Pesta quickly ruled there was no evidence for a mistrial, because Simpson had been dropped from the suit. Somehow this did not surprise me.

Firefighter Simpson had now been dropped from the suit leaving Lt. Jim Sharpe, the four police officers (Frank Cavalieri, Kevin Long, Gordon Gouwens and Theron (Jim) McClain), the State of Florida (they constructed the guardrail also under suspicion), the company that dug the drainage ditch, and the landowner. It's that old cast net theory we mentioned earlier.

Metro Dade Fire Rescue Airport Crash Truck

Chapter Twenty-one

THE PROSECUTION AND THE DEFENSE LINE UP THEIR EXPERT WITNESSES

Attorneys Meyers and Bernstein had contacted Metro Accident Investigator Indy Morgado to examine the evidence gathered at the accident scene.

There were several very important questions that needed to be answered:

1. Was the vehicle traveling at a speed above the legal speed limit?
2. What was the speed limit in that area? If posted it would be 40 miles per hour; if not posted in a rural area it would be 55 miles per hour.
3. What did the 132 feet of skid marks left by the vehicle tell us?
4. Damage to the vehicle would be evidence of the speed of impact.
5. If the guard rail had been installed, would it have helped the accident victims survive?
6. Was the existing guard rail the proper height and was the spacing of the wood supports the proper distance apart?
7. Was the driver legally intoxicated?
8. Was the angle and distance of the swell to the drainage ditch correct by State Standards?

When you start putting things under a magnifying glass you can discover all kinds of cracks, and that was what the Prosecution was hoping for. Something wiggling in that cast net. When the accident investigator contacted the vehicle impound, he found that the vehicle had been put through the shredder. This is not supposed to happen to a vehicle involved in a multiple death accident. Oh well, attorneys are not supposed to join the other side either.

Attorneys Meyers and Bernstein had also contacted Howard Livingston. He had headed the President's Council on Highway Safety and was an expert on road construction and the development of guard rails. We would not see Livingston until we went to court where he would testify.

Metro Accident Investigator Indy Morgado had informed our defense attorneys he had worked out a mathematical formula using the 132 feet of skid marks showing that the vehicle involved in the accident was traveling approximately 60 miles per hour. An the skid marks were actually "hash marks." Hash marks are left by a vehicle that is being held into a turn by centrifugal force. In short, this means that the driver when startled by the oncoming vehicle flashing his lights to warn him, turned back into his lane holding the vehicle in a right turn over-correcting. The hash marks started four feet in the oncoming or eastbound lane and continued 132 feet until they left the roadway on the north side of the west bound lane. This was a very important discovery. Not only did it indicate the speed of the vehicle, but also clearly showed the driver was in the oncoming lane and over-corrected holding the vehicle in a turn until it left the roadway. After leaving the roadway, the vehicle traveled about thirty feet down the swell to where it impacted the vertical limestone wall of the drainage ditch.

The defense attorneys constructed a large poster some four feet high and eight feet in length to show the timeline of the rescue events in detail. The idea here was to clearly show that there had been a delay in reporting the accident.

The exact time the police and fire were dispatched and arrived at the scene. Time the jaws began to free the trapped victims in the vehicle. The time the victims received triage and treatment. The time of transport to appropriate hospitals to treat their injuries. Arrival of police investigators and the medical examiner. This timeline gave indisputable evidence that the fire and police acted in a professional and expedient manner. The timeline chart would be displayed in the courtroom. Little did we know but the prosecution would display a two-foot by four-foot picture of the deceased little three-year-old Nora Lopez in her Sunday dress for the jury to look at during the trial.

Chapter Twenty-two
LAWSUIT GOES TO TRIAL
JURY SELECTION

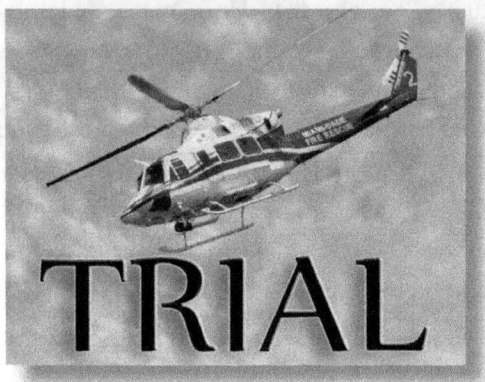

After all the depositions had been taken and the expert witnesses contacted, it was time to select the jury. I, up to that time, had never thought much about jurors, I had been a juror myself many times, but I somehow never connected the two. Of course, I had never been on trial before either. Spending the greater part of my life as a fireman, I thought of myself as a white knight charging forth on a great white horse saving lives and doing good deeds.

It was rather depressing to now be accused of allowing people to drown in a submerged vehicle, handing out matches with gasoline in the ditch, playing catch with dead babies while people died. It was difficult to keep the allegations from migrants separate from my own convictions in the beginning. As time passed, I kept remembering they put their family in that vehicle with a drunk driver, the driver overcorrected the vehicle ending up in the ditch. I responded and did the best job I knew how to do to save the lives of the injured. Those who died, did so in the first few minutes after the fatal crash before I or the police arrived. Nevertheless, here I am on trial for four wrong full deaths.

As the jury selection proceeded, I was amazed at the quality of the jurors. A nurse, a police officer's wife, an executive from Eastern Airlines, a construction worker. The high quality of the six jurors came from the fact that the entire prospective group were all excellent jurors; no one would have been a bad selection.

First Day in Court

ON JUNE 20, 1983, the trial began, our first day in court. I had always said, "If I am going to get (sued), it is going to be for what I did, not what I didn't do." In the months prior to the trial, we met with numerous experts and discussed our rescue efforts at length. Doctor Bop and Doctor Lasey, the police and fire experts for the county, fully agreed that we handled every aspect of the rescue in a manner consistent with the most advance rescue methods in the country.

We received a lot of rhetoric from the department, that the department cannot back you if you fail to follow protocol. Where is this backing now? I never received a phone call from anyone connected to the Metro Fire Department other than my fellow firefighters from the district. The Fire Chief nor any of his staff were even aware that the welfare of my family, my home, my boat, and everything I owned was in danger of being taken away if I lost this lawsuit. I tried to quell these frustrations and fears as we entered the courtroom. I felt a deep sense of personal conviction on the part of my attorneys Sonny Meyers and Ron Bernstein and the entire staff of the County Attorney's Office. I was not alone, the entire County Attorney's Office was supporting us. The firemen in the stations were witnesses so they could not attend but gave their support.

On this first day in court the prosecution began presenting their case to the six jurors. Any illusions that the truth would be spoken by the prosecution was quickly shattered, when the prosecution called the first police officer to take the stand. The prosecuting attorney bellowed, "So you didn't want to get your feet wet, so you let the little three-year-old Nora Lopez drown in the vehicle." The officer in the stand was so shocked he could not answer, not that this off-the-wall statement deserved any answer. Perhaps the horror on the face of the officer on the stand and the rest of the defendants spoke volumes on how they felt. Of course, the prosecution had the two foot by four foot picture of little Nora Lopez in her Sunday dress propped up against their desk so everyone could see it. The prosecution continued to blast the police officers with lies and untruths for the next two days.

Apparently, they felt they could break one of the officers. Their target was Jim McClain. McClain was undergoing a nasty divorce, his soon to be ex-wife was involved with one of the attorneys, and his mother was dying of cancer. McClain is a good officer and a good person I knew him long before this accident. The attorneys for the plaintiff continued to hammer away at McClain, accusing him of hiding under a bridge on the way to the call so he would not be first on the scene. Well, Jim McClain broke down alright. He poured out his heart on the stand about how he always wanted to be a police officer and loved his job helping people, and how he would never do anything that would harm anyone.

After about twenty minutes of the most heartwarming display of emotion you could imagine, the prosecution was wishing they could stick a sock in his mouth and shut him up. Their attempt to discredit the police had backfired in their face. I must say I enjoyed every minute of it!

The attorneys for the plaintiff; Williamson and Smith, obtained their expert witnesses from magazine ads, they had credentials but were obviously programmed to make false statements and to present completely erroneous and misleading information to the jury. Attorneys Williamson and Smith coached their expert witnesses from the table where they were seated. Signaling how to answer the defense's questions. Whenever the defense was making a strong point while questioning the expert witness, the prosecuting attorneys would drop a book from their table or drop their keys on the floor to distract the jury.

Attorneys Williamson and Smith made one lame attempt to soften the fact that the driver was three times legally drunk. They read a letter supposedly from Dr. Ron Wright, the Medical Examiner for Broward County. They actually read the letter together and it went like this: "Yes the driver was intoxicated, but he was getting less intoxicated!"

Ron Wright was one of the best accident scene reconstruction experts in the world. I know for a fact he is not sympathetic to drunk drivers involved in fatal accidents. Ron Wright was not present, and I would bet money on the fact this letter was fraudulent. I attended classes with Ron Wright, he would teach the rescue paramedics to look at the physical evidence in the car to gain insight into possible injuries. Examples would be a bent steering wheel, look for chest and internal injuries. Windshield broken from inside out look for head and neck injuries.

Chapter Twenty-three
THE PROSECUTING ATTORNEY BITES OFF MORE THAN HE CAN CHEW

On several occasions, Attorney Virgin deliberately passed by the table where Lt. Sharpe and Officers Cavalieri, Long, Gouwens McClain, and attorneys for the defense Meyers and Bernstein were seated and made a derogatory remark to Meyers. The first time it was "you're a little shit." The second time Virgin came by and said, "You're a prick." Attorney Meyers asked to sidebar with Judge Pesta and complained about the prosecution's derogatory remarks.

Judge Pesta stated he did not hear the remarks. I guess we would have to wake him up before he could hear anything, yes, he did snooze from time to time. The third time Smith passed by the desk and made a remark to Attorney Meyers, Sonny jumped up on top of the table and ran the length of it landing on Attorney Smith's back and took him to the ground. We pulled Sonny off the shocked Smith and Judge Pesta cleared the room. After the Judge set some ground rules the trial continued. Smith made no more trips past Sonny's desk.

As the trial progressed, the prosecution continued to try and distract the jury whenever the defense was questioning their witness. Sonny suggested that we stand and point each time the prosecuting attorney tried to distract the jury. Lt. Sharpe and the four police officers would stand at their table and point at the Attorneys each time they attempted to distract the jury by dropping books or keys on to the floor.

The attorneys suing us had collected more than eight million dollars in damages for clients in the past year so their antics were not to be taken lightly.

A sign over the judges desk read, "We seek only the truth here." Obviously Judge Pesta and the prosecuting attorneys had not read the sign. We certainly did not see any truth from the plaintiff's side as they continued with unbelievable accusations.

Lt. Sharpe thought to himself, *After eighteen years of serving the citizens of Dade County in a highly professional manner and helping to formulate concepts and procedures designed to save lives, I surely thought the judge or someone would stand up and say STOP. You are insulting Lt. Sharpe and these fine police officers' integrity and honor, but no one did.*

After the grilling of the police officers, the prosecution wanted to ask Lt. Sharpe a question. They said he doesn't have to take the stand he can just stand at the table. Attorney Myers insisted that I take the stand and be sworn in if I was going to answer a question. The question was so meaningless I don't even remember what it was. This seemed very strange. They asked the question, and I sat down. It was time now for the defense to present their side of the case.

Chapter Twenty-four
OUR EXPERT ON HIGHWAY SAFETY ARRIVES

Howard Livingston, our expert on guard rails, roads and highway safety had not arrived yet. It was five o'clock in the afternoon and court was over for that day, but he was scheduled to take the stand the next day. At 5:30 p.m. Livingston walked into the court room, Sonny and Ron were very relieved. He had flown into Miami International Airport, rented a car and drove to the scene of the accident. He was only at the accident scene for about an hour and had found a speed limit sign (40 miles per hour) posted. He had measured the height and distance between supports for the guardrail. The attorneys for the plaintiff were arguing that if the guardrail had been extended to the location of the accident, it would have saved their lives. This would be disputed later in the trial. Livingston had also measured the width and grade of the swell. He also measured the width and depth of the drainage ditch, and tested the firmness of the bottom of the ditch. Lt. Sharpe turned to Sonny and said, "I like this guy; he is a real expert."

Livingston walked over to the large drawing of the swell and drainage ditch and said, "This drawing is all wrong."

Sonny said, "It is the prosecution's version of the scene. The ditch looks like a river, not a ditch barely seven foot wide, the swell is too steep a grade and too narrow. The guardrail is too high, and the supports are too far apart to represent the existing guardrail. At this point I (Lt. Sharpe) felt all warm and fussy about our defense. Our Experts were very knowledgeable and clean cut, Dr. Bop and Dr. Lasey, the experts on police and fire procedures; Indy Morgado our expert on traffic investigation and reconstruction; now Livingston our expert on highway safety, road construction and guardrail construction. Lt. Sharpe was the big gun, an expert in rescues involving multiple victims in rural areas, and in the use of the "jaws of life," one of the best trained and experienced fire department Para medics in the country.

Chapter Twenty-five
THE STAGE WAS NOW SET FOR THE SHOWDOWN

Doctor Bop and Doctor Lasey were our first expert witnesses. They attest to the fact that the Metro Fire and Police Departments are some of the best trained and most experienced Departments in the country. The actions of the police and fire rescue personnel on the scene of this tragic accident were consistent with the most advanced rescue methods in the country. Again, the prosecution dropped books and fumbled with keys in an attempt to distract the jury. Again, Lt. Sharpe and the four police officers said nothing but stood and pointed at the prosecuting attorney's antics. Sonny said it was OK if we made some noise with our chair when coming to a standing position. The jury was very intelligent, and I could not see them buying into these attorney's false accusations, lies and antics. I (Lt. Sharpe) could feel the Jurors eyes watching my every reaction, and they did not hesitate to make eye contact.

Next Indy Morgado our accident investigator and reconstruction expert was to take the stand. He had determined mathematically the approximate speed of the vehicle prior to the impact with the wall of the ditch. He had determined that speed to be 60 miles per hour, based on the distance an arc of 132 feet of "Hash Marks" made by the vehicle as it was held into to a turn. The Hash Marks are made due to centrifugal force, the vehicle wants to travel in a straight line but is being forced to turn.

Howard Livingston had found the speed limit sign that posted the speed of 40 miles per hour. Unfortunately, the vehicle involved in the accident was sent through the crusher before he had a chance to examine it. "It is very unusual that a vehicle involved in an accident claiming four lives and involved in a lawsuit with a hold on it for evidence would be destroyed. It is also unusual that all the pictures from the scene showing beer cans in the front seat were lost, but pictures showing baby bottles floating in the ditch were recovered. All of the police and fire tapes of the radio transmissions were also lost. In short, thanks to our accident investigator, we had established that:

1. The vehicle was traveling at a speed of 60 miles per hour
2. The posted speed limit was 40 miles per hour
3. The vehicle was four feet in the oncoming lane (eastbound lane) of traffic and continued across the westbound lane down the swell and to the point of impact with the ditch.

Howard Livingston our highway safety and guardrail expert was to take the stand next to testify as an expert witness for the defense. He was a small man in stature but reminded me of everybody's favorite grandfather. Gold rim glasses and thick eyebrows resembling the wise old owl. By contrast the prosecutions expert witnesses looked like criminals just released from jail with shady eyes and dark oily hair.

Attorney Meyers asked Livingston about the prosecutions drawing of the scene of the accident. Livingston stated that the ditch was only seven feet wide, but the prosecution's drawing made it appear more like a river, and the grade and width is incorrect on the swell. "It's my opinion, and judging from the testimony heard here in the courtroom as to the extensive damage to the front and rear of the vehicle, it struck the wall of the ditch then flipped end over end impacting the rear of the vehicle on the ground then came to rest in the ditch on its roof some thirty feet from the initial point of impact."

Attorney Meyers asked, "In relation to the guardrail, the plaintiff's state that the victims' lives would have been saved if the guardrail had been extended just one hundred feet more."

Livingston referred to the guard rail in the prosecutions drawing of the scene, "This drawing is incorrect. The height of the guard rail is eighteen inches, and the vertical supports are twenty-four inches apart. This guard rail is designed correctly according to state standards."

Attorney Meyers asked if the guard rail had been extended past the accident scene would it have saved the lives of the victims?

Livingston said, "The answer is no; guard rails are constructed to withstand an impact angle of not more than 15 degrees from a mid-size car with an average bumper height of fourteen inches above the ground. In this case the vehicle involved a Chevrolet Suburban is a very heavy vehicle, almost one third more weight than a mid-size car, and the bumper height in more like eighteen inches above the ground. The additional weight of the vehicle, height of the bumper and greater angle of impact would actually result in more injuries to the victims."

Attorney Meyers inquired, "Why more injuries?"

Livingston said, "The guardrail would have caused the vehicle to flip into the air on impact with the guard rail."

The attorneys for the plaintiff seemed to be running out of books to drop and keys to rattle and the jury seemed to be impressed by our knowledgeable and experienced expert witnesses.

The cross examination by the prosecution was weak, it seemed they didn't know how to cope with the knowledge and experience being presented in the court room. Their earlier attacks and accusations on the police officers seemed to have exposed their soft under side to the jury.

Well, the last big gun was still waiting to be called to the witness stand. Lt. Sharpe is the most experienced and best trained rescue officer on the department. Skilled in rescue operations with multiple victims in rural areas. He had taught the use of the "jaws of life" and used them for more than fifteen years. This was the defense attorney's chance to launch an attack on the prosecution that they had no defense against. Lt. Sharpe handled the rescue from start to finish and the experts agree he had used the most advance medical rescue techniques in the country to save these patients lives.

Lt. Sharpe was beginning to feel the pressure, attorney Smith sat right across from him on purpose at their table reading the manual for the "jaws of life." Lt. Sharpe leaned over to Sonny and said, "You know I don't think I remember everything in that manual even though I have probably cut over a thousand people out of cars and planes."

Sonny said, "Remember, he is only reading the manual, he has never used the jaws. He is just trying to rattle your cage mentally." This seemed to be what the prosecution had been trying to do all along, distort the truth with lies in order to have us believe they were telling the truth.

It was a scary thought, but I was beginning to understand their logic or lack of it.

Sonny had me study attorney Smith "questioning rhythm" though out the trial. He would coach me, "Watch; first question is very easy, second question a little harder, third question also easy, fourth question very easy, fifth question he would slam you: 'you didn't want to get down in the ditch, so you let them drown didn't you?'"

Sonny told me, when you take the stand, adjust your chair to the right a little so you are looking directly at the jury, make eye contact. When Smith starts his rhythm of questions, it allows him to proceed to the third or fourth question then make him repeat the question just before he hits you with the big question. If it bothers him make him repeat it again.

It was now time for Lt. Sharpe to take the stand, Attorneys Myers and Bernstein and the four police officers had been waiting for this moment. Lt. Sharpe was beyond reproach by the prosecution's accusations and attacks. His actions from the beginning of the rescue to the end were well documented, he was not involved in crowd control or searching for the missing driver of the vehicle, only the attempts to save the lives of the people in the vehicle.

Attorney Meyers stated for the court he was calling Lt. Sharpe to the witness stand. The attorneys for the prosecution jumped up from their seats and stated, "Oh no, Your Honor, we have already had Lt. Sharpe take the stand."

Now I understood why the prosecution had me stand and answer that seemingly stupid question much earlier in the proceedings. Sonny lost it; screaming at the Judge, "Lt. Sharpe stands to lose everything he owns in this lawsuit and you are not going to let him take and stand in his own defense?"

My faithful wife had been in the court room every day and had maintained her cool even in the face of all these false accusations and lies. When the prosecution tried to keep me from taking the stand, she knew the limit of her patience had been reached. Rather than blow up and start screaming at the Judge and the prosecution, she made the decision to exit the court room to cool off. When she reached the exit doors of the court, one of the double doors was locked and one was open. Well she hit the locked door and woke up the entire court room with a thunderous bang. Even Judge Pesta was awake. Successfully navigating the open door, she left the court room to cool down.

Judge Pesta seeming to grasp the explosive nature of the situation and ordered the courtroom cleared once again. Judge Pesta and the attorneys, came to an agreement that Lt. Sharpe would take the stand after a long and heated debate from the prosecution on the matter. It seemed that the prosecution felt their best defense was to keep Lt. Sharpe from testifying.

Chapter Twenty-six
LT. SHARPE TAKES THE STAND

Court reconvened, and Lt. Sharpe took the stand. I adjusted the chair to the right as Sonny had directed so I could look the jury right in the eye. The jury seemed to be pleased with that. Attorney Smith started his dog and pony show asking his first questions from the manual of the "jaws of life." Sure, enough the rhythm was true to form, three or four easy questions and then the blast question. The questions went like this, as best I can remember.

Attorney Smith: The jaws run on gasoline?

Lt. Sharpe: Yes.

Attorney Smith: Are they hydraulically powered?

Lt. Sharpe: Yes.

Attorney Smith: The head of the jaws weighs about fifty pounds?

Lt. Sharpe, that is correct.

Attorney Smith: You couldn't get the jaws started because you ran out of gas! Is that correct?

Lt. Sharpe: Your Honor, I didn't understand the question. Could Attorney Smith repeat it please?

Sonny was correct; this would get to Smith quickly, His face turned blood red and the veins in his face were protruding.

Attorney Smith: You couldn't get the jaws started because you ran out of gas?

Lt. Sharpe: Your Honor, I still do not understand the question.

Judge Pesta: Sharpe, you will answer the question.

Lt. Sharpe: Your Honor, I don't understand the question because we never ran out of gas and had no trouble starting the jaws of life. They are started every morning when the truck is checked out at shift change.

The jury seemed to grasp the humor in my exchange, after all I had sat quietly in the court room while this asshole made one false accusation and lie after another, dropped books and rattled keys to distract the jury. Now it was our turn. Sonny had a serious look on his face, like don't take this too far. After watching Smith study the jaws manual, I will have to admit I had reservations before taking the stand.

I was feeling confident now, perhaps the great white shark, as Smith is known, might be a mullet in a room full of sharks.

The second round of questions followed the same pattern.

Attorney Smith: the vehicle was upside down in the water?

Lt. Sharpe: Yes, it landed on its roof in the drainage ditch.

Attorney Smith: You walked across the vehicle to reach the other side of the water?

Lt. Sharpe: Yes, that is correct.

Attorney Smith: At this point you surveyed the damage to the vehicle!

Lt. Sharpe: Correct.

Attorney Smith: Did you realize you were pushing the vehicle down into the water drowning the people inside?

Attorney Meyers: Objection, leading the witness!

Judge Pesta: Rephrase the question.

Attorney Smith: Did the car sink down while you were standing on it?

Lt. Sharpe: Could you repeat the question?

Attorney Smith with a very red face: Your Honor I think Lt. Sharpe needs a hearing aid.

Lt. Sharpe: I am sorry Your Honor but the last fifteen years of sirens and air horns on those fire trucks have affected my hearing somewhat. Please repeat the question.

Attorney Smith: In a much louder voice, did the car sink down while you were standing on it?

Lt. Sharpe: No, the vehicle was sitting on a bed of limestone rock and we were monitoring the stability of the vehicle during the rescue.

Attorney Smith continued the questioning but having to stop and repeat the last question was destroying his rhythm and shock factor.

Attorney Smith: Did you notice a small gap in the upper part of the back door of the vehicle?

Lt. Sharpe: Yes, I did.

Attorney Smith: Was this a failed attempt by the fire department to pry open the door.

Lt. Sharpe: No, this opening was not made by the fire department.

Attorney Smith: Is it true that this failed attempt to pry open the back door delayed the rescue of people trapped inside the car.

Lt. Sharpe: I am sorry, but could you repeat the question? I don't understand the question.

Attorney Smith now looked like he was going to have a stroke. His face was purple red, veins protruding and yelling at the top of his lungs.

Attorney Smith: Is it true that this failed attempt to pry open the back door delayed the rescue of people trapped inside the car?

Lt. Sharpe: The small opening in the back door was made by migrant workers trying to pry open the door to free the victims prior to calling the fire and police departments. Yes, this did cause a delay of perhaps thirty minutes, getting fire rescue on scene with proper equipment.

Judge Pesta, now very awake, responded: Lt. Sharpe just answer the question.

At this point Attorney Smith had been effectively neutralized; his blast and shock question had been interrupted by my repeatedly asking him to repeat the question. This interruption also gave me the time to regain composure and think about my answer. Attorney Williamson took over the questioning but was not as affective as Smith could have been. An attorney with little or no training in emergency medicine, rescue techniques and extrication of victims from a vehicle in a canal does not due well against experience and training.

Lt. Sharpe is questioned by the defense

This was the moment we had been waiting for; it was time for Lt. Sharpe to tell the real story to the jury. It would appear that the jury had a belly full of the prosecutions dog and pony show and was hungry for some real information.

Attorney Meyers stepped up to the stand and the defense began their questions. I felt vindicated, I had survived the attack of the "great white shark" and lost very little blood. Now we could get down to the truth.

Attorney Meyers: Lt. Sharpe when and how did you receive the rescue call on alarm number 02615 on January 13, 1980?

Lt. Sharpe: Rescue 6 was in quarters at 288 Street and Biscayne Drive (288th Street Southwest) We received the call by radio at 20:33 (8:33 p.m.) from the Metro Dade Fire and Rescue Alarm Office a 317 (auto accident) an occupied vehicle in the canal at 13352

71

SW 314th Street the South Dade Labor Camp. While answering the radio, I requested verification of the address, there is no canal at this location.

Attorney Meyers: What other units were dispatched?

Lt. Sharpe: Engine 16 was in route from Krome Ave. and northwest 3rd Street in Homestead in route. I requested additional units Rescue 16 and Metro Diver.

Attorney Meyers: What did you find when you arrived?

Lt. Sharpe: We took 137th Avenue South, that was the general location of most of the canals in the area. The alarm office corrected the address to 312th Street and southwest 137th Avenue. On arrival at the given address, we could see red lights about ½ mile west on 312th Street. We corrected the address for incoming units.

Attorney Meyers: Continue what did you observed on arrival at the scene.

Lt. Sharpe: Rescue 6 arrived at the Metro Police location and weaved through several cars stopped at the scene locating the rescue about 40 feet short of the vehicle in the ditch. I wanted to keep the area clear in the road next to the accident for our triage area. The approximate time was 20:39 (8:39 pm) the time of our arrival. As I exited the rescue truck, I observed about fifteen migrants standing on or about the vehicle in the ditch. The smell of gasoline was very strong as I approached the vehicle. Metro Police were attempting to control an intoxicated and unruly crowd. The police asked the intoxicated migrates to extinguish their cigarettes, they refused.

Attorney Meyers: Explain to the jury the position of the vehicle in the ditch.

Lt. Sharpe: I descended the 8–10-foot swell area down to the drainage ditch. I observed a late model Chevrolet Suburban, wheels up, facing east. I observed extensive damage to the front and rear of the vehicle, the hood was bent downward blocking the front windshield and the entire front appeared to be set back about three feet. The south side of the vehicle rested firmly against the wall of the drainage ditch. I observed the ditch to be continuous with no point of crossing. I crossed over the vehicle and observed and ascertained that it rested solidly between the north and south walls of the ditch. I further noted that it rested firmly on the bottom of the ditch which appeared to be solid rock. The vehicle rested slightly lower in the southeast corner and slightly higher in the northwest corner. The water level was noted by this officer and observed during the rescue operation, no change occurred.

I stepped to the bank on the north side and observed a patient ten feet northeast of the auto lying on the bank. The patient was conscious and orientated with a fractured right femur and was a female (approximately age 50) possibly from the car. I reassured her help was on the way and not to move. At this point I assigned paramedic Simpson to evaluate her injuries. The west end of the vehicle (the rear end) displayed high-speed deceleration damage, patients would have to exit along a hazardous path, submerging underwater through baby carriages and other paraphernalia. I advised Battalion 9 now in route of the situation and requested additional manpower and equipment.

The jury seemed to be glued to every word.

Attorney Meyers: Lt. Sharpe, please continue.

Lt. Sharpe: I determined entry with the jaws would be the most expeditious entry, ordering firefighter Simpson to enter through the rear door would be too risky. On the north side there was an eroded area in the bank giving access to a small part of the door. One of the migrants told me four or five people were inside and they had unsuccessfully tried to pry the door with a crowbar. The small opening made by this prying allowed me to see inside the vehicle. Two to seven people very excited could be heard banging in the front and rear seat area of the vehicle. I reassured the migrants that the fire department was on the scene, and we were going to have them out of there in just minutes. At 20:43 (8:43 p.m.) I observed through the aforementioned opening that there was two to three feet of air space inside the vehicle. At this point Engine 16 and Rescue 16 arrived carrying the jaws.

Attorney Meyers: Lt. Sharpe, explain to the jury how you gained entry into the vehicle.

Lt. Sharpe: I assigned paramedic McVey to assist Simpson with the injured lady on the bank while I conferred with Lt. Easely from Rescue 16 and Lt. Hendricks of Engine 16. We agreed the north rear door was the best location for entry. I assigned two members of Engine 16's crew to explore alternate means of entry while the driver and tail board man from Engine 16 readied the jaws for operation.

Attorney Meyers: Was the crowd a factor in the operation?

Lt. Sharpe: Yes, they were. A crowd of 15 or 20 migrants on the north side of the ditch impeded our rescue efforts by standing in the way and when they were told to leave, they would only retreat into the bushes to return shortly and be right back in the way again. There were at least this many migrants on the roadway on the south side of the ditch.

Attorney Meyers: Continue to tell the jury about the rescue effort.

Lt. Sharpe: At 20:45 (8:45 p.m.) Engine 6 arrived I assigned Engine 6 to light the area with their generator and area lights while the other half of the crew readied backboards and medical equipment to the triage area set up on the roadway. At approximately 20:49 (8:49 pm) the rear north door was opened by the jaws. The lady found on the north bank had been moved on a backboard to the triage area and was being treated by paramedics.

I assigned Simpson to enter the vehicle through the north rear door and evaluate patients for extrication (two firefighters assisting) and treatment in the triage area. Lt. Hendricks and the crew of Engine 16 began removal of the north front door. Simpson had to remove one patient before he could enter the north rear door of the vehicle. Lt. Hendricks now had the front door open and Engine 6 and Engine 16's crew began transporting the injured to the triage area.

Attorney Meyers: OK, the doors have been opened by the jaws; what happened next?

Lt. Sharpe: The water level inside the car had showed no change during the rescue, now we had firefighters inside the vehicle with the patients. Simpson now in the area between the front and rear seat reported 45s (dead patients) and asked should he start removing them. I answered no, remove the injured patients first. We already had a serious crowd control problem, to bring dead children out of the vehicle would start a panic. I advised metro police of the D.O.A.s (dead on arrival) and requested more crowd control. As I departed the vehicle and started up the swell next to the road a migrant came screaming down the embankment and jumped on to Lt. Hendricks back. Hendricks was carrying a patient on a backboard at the time. Hendricks managed not to drop the patient but hurt his back. The migrant was removed from the scene and placed in a patrol car. All the patients from the vehicle were coated with gasoline and oil and were difficult to keep on the backboards. At the triage area, patients were cleaned to minimize chemical burns from the oil and gas.

Attorney Meyers: What type of injuries did the patients from the vehicle have?

Lt. Sharpe: At the triage area I observed the first two or three patients. Most had gross insult, high-speed deceleration trauma injuries, multiple fractures and lacerations, possible internal injuries, and compound fractures with gross angulations.

Attorney Meyers: What type of treatment did these patients receive?

Lt. Sharpe: The extrication continued at the vehicle, in the triage area paramedics began the second stage evaluating patients, stabilizing the most critical life-threatening injuries first and less critical injuries second. The paramedics started IVs with ringer's lactate and 18 gauge catheters to stabilizing patients with low blood pressures and deployed the MAST suit when necessary. Stabilized fractures with splints, stopped bleeding and cleaned and bandaged open wounds. All patients with head trauma got neck braces to guard against possible neck fractures. The time is 20:58 (8:58 p.m.).

Attorney Meyers: For the information of the jury, what is the MAST suit?

Lt. Sharpe: The MAST suit was developed by the military. It is a rubber inflatable suit, similar to a pair of rubber pants, that can be blow up using air pressure. The pants fit from the ankle to the waist and the upper part of the suit covers from the waist to the upper chest. It can be placed under the patient and fastens together with Velcro around the legs and the chest. The benefit of the MAST suit is the Tampa nodding of the area auto-transfuses 1200 cc of fluid (plasma) from the legs into the chest in a matter of minutes where the vital organs are and protects them. The MAST suit also controls bleeding and acts as a soft splint to badly angulated fractures.

Attorney Meyers: Lt. Sharpe what was the next step in the rescue attempt?

Lt. Sharpe: The patients needed to be transported to the nearest hospitals that could handle their type of injuries, and I needed to know how many patients each hospital could treat without overloading their staff. I contacted med com by telemetry radio and requested that Coral Reef General Hospital and James Archer Smith Hospital be placed simultaneously on a single channel. Med com advised the med channel and approval. This radio connection placed me in direct voice contact with the emergency room staff of each hospital. I advised the two hospitals that we had a 317 (auto accident) a vehicle upside down in a drainage ditch on southwest 312th Street and 135th Avenue with 13 victims.

The description followed: approximately nine serious to critical, three DOA and one unknown. I requested that they ascertain and advise me the number and type of patients that each hospital could handle.

74

Attorney Meyers: Tell the jury how the patients were divided among the hospitals.

Lt. Sharpe: The paramedics in the triage area began reporting to me the extent and nature of each of the patients' injuries so that collectively we could establish a priority for transport and the hospital that could best treat the patients type of injuries. Time now approximately 21:10 (9:10 p.m.). Each patient received a tag detailing the injuries and the hospital to be transported to. Lt. Cockeran, from Engine 6, was appointed load master. He was responsible for loading and dispatching each patient or patients to the assigned hospital as they were loaded aboard the transport rescues and ambulances.

Attorney Meyers: At approximately what time were all the injured victims from the vehicle transported?

Lt. Sharpe: At approximately 21:38 all patients had been transported from the scene. Patients transported to James Archer Smith Hospital in Homestead had a fifteen-minute transport time, but patients transported to Coral Reef Hospital had a 45-to-50 minute transport time. Coral Reef Hospital is located on southwest 152nd Street just west of US 1.

Attorney Meyers: So in a little less that one hour after your arrival on the scene, all of the patients were extricated from the vehicle in the ditch, transported up the swell to the triage area, stabilized and then transported to local hospitals.

Lt. Sharpe: That is correct.

Attorney Meyers: Ladies and gentlemen of the jury, that is remarkable.

Attorney Smith: Objection, Your Honor.

Attorney Meyers: Lt. Sharpe, your job was not over at this point.

Lt. Sharpe: That is correct, we still had the grim job of removing the dead children from the vehicle. At this point we had an adequate number of police on the scene to control the intoxicated and unruly crowd. The injured patients whose lives had hung in the balance had been transported to the hospital and were receiving treatment. The crowd of more than 150 migrants would not affect their well-being. One by one the lifeless bodies of the dead children was brought on a backboard from the vehicle up the swell where they were wrapped in a yellow blanket. The driver at this time had not been discovered, he would be discovered trapped in the wreckage when the vehicle was removed from the ditch.

Seven firemen were treated for chemical burns from the gasoline and oil after the scene was secured. The 45s were released to the Medical Examiner and the scene secured by the fire department and turned over to Metro Police and Metro Police Diver for body recovery and homicide investigation.

Rescue 6 returned to service at 23:15 and began restocking the truck with supplies in order to be ready for the next call.

Attorney Meyers: Thank you, Lt. Sharpe, that will be all. You can return to your seat.

Chapter Twenty-seven
ATTORNEY FOR THE DEFENSE
GIVES HIS CLOSING REMARKS

A ttorney Meyers in Summary displayed the large 4-foot by 8-foot "time chart" showing the time the police and fire were dispatched and arrived.

The time Lt. Sharpe on Rescue 6 assumed command of the scene. The time the jaws opened the first door and then the second door. The time the patients were extricated, and treatment began. The time the patients were transported to the local hospital for further treatment. The time the scene was secured.

Sonny then summed up the testimony of our expert witnesses' testimony. Dr. Bop and Dr. Lasey, experts on fire rescue and police, testified that the Metro Fire and Rescue and Metro Police departments were some of the best trained and most experienced departments in the county. The methods used during the rescue attempt were consistent with the most advanced methods in the country.

Indy Morgado established the speed of the vehicle using a mathematical formula based on the length and ark of the Hash Marks. The Hash Marks showed clearly the fact the vehicle was in the oncoming lane of traffic and then was held into a turn until impact with the ditch. The vehicle was traveling at 60 miles per hour. The posted speed limit is 40 miles per hour.

Howard Livingston disputed the fact that extending the guard rail would have saved lives, stating for the record that guardrails are designed for moderate size cars impacting the rail at a 15 degrees angle or less. The higher bumper of the suburban and greater angle of impact would have caused more injuries in the vehicle. He also corrected the prosecution's drawing on the guardrail and the drainage ditch. He further stated the guardrail and swell area were properly designed by State Standers.

Lt. Sharpe, the fire officer in charge of the scene, gave you the jury a step-by-step analysis of the actions taken at the scene to save the lives of the accident victims. His description of events left no room for speculation as to the experience and training of the fire rescue crews on the scene of the accident. Ladies and gentlemen of the jury, I say to you that these policemen and firefighters preformed their duties to the best of their ability, and they were not negligent in any way.

When you go behind closed doors to deliberate their fate, I would like for you to ask yourself just one question. If you were trapped in a ditch in an upside down vehicle, partially submerged in water in the black of night, who would you want to arrive on the scene? I rest my case, Your Honor!

Chapter Twenty-eight
THE JURY DELIBERATES

T he jury looked directly at Lt. Sharpe and the four police officers at the table but showed no expression. The judge began to outline for the jury the procedure in a case of this nature. He stated if you find Lt. Sharpe and the four police officers negligent, you must fill in the blanks and decide by what percentage they are negligent. The judge also informed the jury that if they wanted to review any of the evidence in the case, they could ask for it and it would be provided. The jury seemed to understand the proceedings and retired to the deliberation room to deliberate the case.

This was the moment of truth, the moment we had been preparing for for several years. Our faith was in the hands of six jurors, they would decide if the plaintiffs would take away everything we had worked for our homes, cars, boats, and savings. Although I had a lot of faith in the jury, I definitely had a large lump in my throat. I knew we had done no wrong, but had we convinced the jury of that fact? Sonny and Ron both agreed this was an outstanding jury, but they were very hard to read. There was nothing to do now but wait for the jury's decision. When several hours had passed, Sonny was undecided as to whether this was a good sign or a bad sign. We were just hanging around in the hallway passing the time when the officer of the court announced the jury had reached a verdict.

We all filed back into the court room and took our seats. The judge asked the foreman of the jury if they had reached a verdict.

He stated, "Yes, Your Honor, we have."

The judge asked the jury, "How do you find the defendants?"

"Not guilty Your Honor so say we all."

Attorney's Meyers and Bernstein filed to have the other three wrongful death cases dropped and in time they were dropped. It is hard to describe the feeling of being finally exonerated of the charges of killing four people, three of which were children and mistreating nine other badly injured patients. Even though you know in your heart of hearts that you did everything possible to save their lives, it still weighs heavy on your heart.

Walking out of the courthouse that day, the sun seamed unusually bright, the sky a clear blue and the air fresh. It was finally over. We could get back to the job of saving lives and fighting fires without that black cloud hanging over our heads. We had spent more than three years fighting this case. A case that should never have gone to court. These men should never have had to endure the punishment that the prosecuting attorneys heaped on them in pursuit of the almighty dollar.

My wife was confident the entire time that we would prevail, but I was not so sure after seeing the truth distorted so badly in that courtroom. I can still see that sign in my mind's eye that was posted over the judge's desk, "We seek only the truth in this court room." Thankfully other people involved in rescue efforts will not have to endure this kind of abuse thanks to the "Good Samaritan Act" passed just two weeks after this terrible accident occurred.

Chapter Twenty-nine
"THE GOOD SAMARITAN ACT"

Negligence Chapter 768

1.13 Good Samaritan Act; immunity from civil liability.

(1)   This act shall be known and cited as the "Good Samaritan Act."

(2)   Any person, including those licensed to practice medicine, who gratuitously and in good faith renders emergency care or treatment at the scene of an emergency outside of a hospital, doctors office, or other place having proper medical equipment, without objection of the injured victim or victims thereof, shall not be held liable for any civil damages as a result of such care or treatment or as a result of any act or failure to act in providing or arranging further medical treatment where the person acts as an ordinary reasonably prudent man would have acted under the same or similar circumstances.

In short, if this accident had occurred just two weeks later, this lawsuit could not have been filed without proving gross negligence on the part of the rescuers.

The County Attorney's Office filed suit against the law firm that suited us and collected $80,000 for the cost of defending the suit against the police and fire department. I asked Sonny if I could send Smith a large jar of Vaseline but he didn't think that was appropriate.

I continued riding rescue with Metro Dade Fire Department for the next ten years, commuting from Cudjoe Key in the Florida Keys. This was an approximate two- and one-half hour drive from home to the fire station. I continued to work shifts with 24 hours on duty and off 48 hours or every third day. My home in the Keys was located right on the ocean, and I continued to operate our charter fishing business *Sea Boots* Charters on Summerland Key just five minutes away from home.

To give you a better perspective of the location; Cudjoe Key is closer to Cuba (89 miles) than it is to Islamorada (90 miles) or 132 miles from Miami on an island in the Florida Straits. My fellow firefighters always thought that I would sooner or later be destroyed by a hurricane. Little did we know what hurricane Andrew, a category five storm, had in store for Homestead, Florida City and South Miami in 1992. More about Hurricane Andrew later.

Chapter Thirty
CHANGES IN FIREFIGHTING
AND MEDICAL RESCUES

Firefighting was changing fast with the advent of larger trucks, better water supply, improved fire inspections and pre-fire planning. We were so busy fighting fires and running rescues in the 1970's and early 1980's we didn't have the time or the manpower to inspect building and prevent a fire from ever happening. We didn't have the time to preplan buildings so when a fire occurred, we were familiar with the layout and dangers of the structure. In the mid 1980's Metro Dade Fire had increased from just 40 firefighters covering 2000 square miles of territory to 600 or 700 firefighters and nearly 40 fire stations. Building inspection became a daily routine. Fire hydrant maintenance and flushing also improved. Today Metro Dade Fire and Rescue has over 90 fire stations and 3000 firefighters.

Well Rescues

ONE OF THE EARLIEST pre-planned rescues was Well Rescues in the south end of the county. The farmers drilled wells in the coral rock approximately 12 inches in diameter to a depth of 10 or 12 feet. The farmers would drop a hard suction hose down into the well and supply water to large irrigation pumps to water the crops.

These wells were often grown over in the fields and small children could accidentally slip into the open wells. Families would enter the fields to pick vegetables with small children and the hidden wells become potential death traps. Captain Dave Frame set up a "Well Rescue Kit" and a procedure for handling these rescues. The first step was to keep people away from the well after the child fell into one. People trying to help would kick the loose gravel and rock down into the well and suffocate the child. Usually, the child would be lodged down about eight feet below the ground level and would have air to breath for the short term. The well kit consisted of a large piece of plywood with a circle cut out of the center this acted as a platform from which to work preventing the loose gravel and dirt from entering the well. A long stiff tube was lowered into the well to supply plenty of oxygen to the child. If we were lucky, sometimes we could use the long boat hook to reach down and snare the child's clothing.

Sometimes you could pull them out but rarely. The boat hook did prevent the child from slipping deeper into the well. A large ditch digger usually supplied by Florida Power and Light or local contractor was brought in to dig a ditch about two feet away from the well down to just below the depth of the child. After the ditch was completed, firefighters would tunnel by hand horizontally over to the well and rescue the child by pulling them through the tunnel into the ditch and out of the ground. This rescue had to be performed perfectly to achieve success and it saved many young children's lives.

Simply securing the area around the well and using the plywood platform bought the firefighters time to dig the ditch and tunnel over to the trapped child. To prevent further accidents children under the age of five are not allowed into the fields and many of the wells have covers today.

Techniques Used in Fighting Fires

A GOOD AGGRESSIVE well-trained crew and a quick response time is a fireman's best defense against fire. In the early 1970s I was a driver engineer on a pumper at Station 19 located just off northwest Seventh Avenue and 131st Street in North Miami. My crew consisted of two other firefighters and myself. There were no officers on many of the trucks during these years and the senior firefighter was in charge. Chet Borger was my shotgun man, we called him the silver fox because of his premature silver hair. We usually had a younger firefighter in training as the third man on the crew. Chet and I had worked together for a number of years and we took pride in fast response times and knowing our territory.

Now a fast response time didn't mean driving at a high rate of speed to the fire or rescue although we did not let any grass grow under our feet. A fast response comes from clearing the fire station very quickly and choosing the most direct route to the scene. We generally cleared the station in less than twenty seconds during the day and 40 seconds at night when we were sleeping. Generally, our third man at night would sleep in the jump seat behind the cab of the truck for fear he would get left at the station when an alarm came in. We accomplished these fast responses by recognizing the tones when they came over the radio, knowing which ones were going to include our unit. When we heard our tone, we immediately got in the truck, and I started the engine and began to roll down the ramp to the street. By the time the assignment was given over the radio we were already responding. The fire trucks assigned to the emergency over the radio told us which direction in general the alarm was going. This gave us a big jump on the other responding units, and we would often beat them into their own territory.

With fires, time is the most important factor, they expand exponentially. We knew that after 11:00 at night most people are sleeping, and time was even more important.

While still a North Miami Fireman, prior to the Metro Dade take over, we had one very important fire call. All calls are important, but this one landed some extra points on our retirement package and saved two lives. In the City of North Miami there are two areas that are very difficult to find addresses in; one is Key Stone Point and the other is San Souci. Our training officer with the city required us to memorize the streets, their location and hydrant locations. Once a year we would have to sit down and fill out a blank map with street names and hydrant locations in both areas.

It was just after midnight when this particular alarm came in, the alarm office barked, "A fully involved apartment on the third floor with people trapped inside." That will get your heart pumping right out of a dead sleep. We responded quickly knowing there was about to be a BBQ, and we were invited. I took back all those bad names I had for our training officer when he used to make us fill out those blank maps. We responded directly to the address and were first to arrive; sure enough the alarm office was not exaggerating this apartment was a ball of fire, the windows on the front of the apartment were broken out and flames were rolling over the roof of this three story building.

We had trained many times for fires in this type of building. These three-story apartment buildings have no back doors, with a living room and kitchen in the front of the apartment and a bedroom and bath in the rear of the apartment. I always carried a 100-foot piece of rope in my bunker coat. As I ran up the stairs to the walkway in front of the apartment, I checked to make sure it was there. When I reached the third floor and the apartment, I lowered the rope to the waiting crew below and they tied a 1½ jump line on to the end of the rope.

I quickly pulled the hose line up because it was getting hot as the flames rolled along the underside of the open hallway next to the fire. I was in full bunker gear with self-contained mask, fire helmet and gloves. The line was charged, and I kicked in the door (already burned in half) and entered the fire keeping low to avoid the steam from the 60-degree fog screen of water I was shooting into the ceiling. The idea here is to use the intense heat of the fire to turn the fog screen into steam and extinguish the fire. If done the way I was trained there would be no water on the floor only light steam on the ceiling and walls. I quickly extinguished the fire and began a search of the apartment. I could hear other firefighters in the apartment now; they had followed my hose line in to assist. A search of the bed, under the bed and closet produced no people. I could only feel my way around the bedroom, and I found a door most likely the bathroom door.

I could hear at least two people banging and screaming on the other side of the closed door. The smoke was still very heavy and muffled the sound. Talking through my mask I asked how many are in there; two they answered. I reassured them the fire was out and we were evacuating the smoke with large attic fans. I told them to stay put. I would return with bunker coats and masks to bring them out. When I returned I was glad I brought bunker coats because the young lady was nude, and you know how firemen are they would peak. Now I had lots of help, we brought the two victims out of the apartment into the fresh air at the end of the open hallway. They told me when they woke up, the living room and kitchen were fully involved between them and the only doors out of the apartment. The window in the rear of the apartment was thirty feet above the ground. They ran into the bathroom and packed wet towels around and under the door and turned on the shower. They were overwhelmed with emotion knowing full well without the quick response and actions of the firefighters, they would have been history. As I talked with the gentleman, after all the excitement had calmed down, I realized that he was a city council member and one that was opposing better equipment and better pension benefits for the fire department.

I looked him in the eye and said, "I would like to ask two favors of you."

He asked, "What's that?"

I said, "Get a new apartment, one with a back door and fire escape, and vote for the equipment and benefits we badly need.

He looked me in the eye and said, "I give you my personal guarantee you will get those wishes."

Chapter Thirty-one
CLOT BUSTERS, TRAUMA UNITS AND HELICOPTER TRANSPORTS

Working as a fireman in a large metropolitan area like Miami is challenging to say the least. Improvement in medicine, transport capability and specialty hospitals made our job so much easier. I was riding Rescue 16 in Homestead when one of the first clot busters was put on the rescue truck to be used in the field. There had been a lot of concern about using the clot busting medication in the field. Some doctors felt the jar of hitting a railroad track after giving a patient the drug could cause the patient to bleed out internally. Others were unsure of the fireman's ability to screen the recipients properly. You had to make sure of the patient's history; recent surgery, or ulcers could cause the patient to bleed out internally.

These clot busting medications dissolved the blood clots in the body and would place a compromised patient's life in grave danger. So several of the rescues in the county were given the clot busters as a trial. We only had the medication a couple of days when we were called to a construction site for a 45-year-old male complaining sudden onset of chest pain. Upon questioning the patient, he had no history of ulcers or surgeries and was the perfect candidate for the drug. We started an IV and administered the clot busting drug just a few minutes later the patient had no more pain and felt fine. We transported to James Archer Smith Hospital where he later walked out with no damage to his heart after suffering a massive M.I. (Myocardial Infarction—heart attack). Previously we could only give oxygen, and medications to prevent dysrhythmias; this was a whole new ball game.

The advent of trauma level hospitals was somewhat painful in the beginning. At first, every major hospital in Dade County put in helicopter landing pads and trauma centers. Then they figured out the majority of level one trauma patients cannot pay their hospital bills and have long stays in the hospital. Soon there was only Jackson Memorial Ryder Trauma Center and Miami Children's Hospital. These are two of the finest hospitals in the country. Both are training hospitals and that is where I received most of my training.

The next step was to improve the medical transportation system. In order for a trauma center to give quality lifesaving treatment, the patient must be received in less than one hour after the injury occurred. This is known as the "Golden Hour." If surgeons can get inside the patient in that first hour, they have an 80 or 90 percent better chance of saving the patient's life. If a patient is received after the Golden Hour, vital organs begin to shut down and the patient's chances for recovery decrease rapidly.

Once a patient is labeled a level one trauma patient, he or she must be received by the trauma center within the hour.

Metro Dade Firefighters Battle a fire caused by a broken gas main

In Dade County with the advent of the medical helicopter transport, the patient will be transported directly from the scene of the accident to the appropriate trauma center. Land transport could only be used for non-trauma patients or patients that were no more than twenty minutes land transport from the trauma center. Transport by air rescue helicopter is not cheap; the average transport will cost from $10,000 to 20,000 dollars per patient. In some areas, private helicopter transport is used. These companies talk the talk by fail to walk the walk. These patients are transported from the scene, by land transport to a local hospital then inter-hospital transfer by private helicopter is arranged.

The problem here is the golden hour is lost, and possibly the patient, if he or she is a trauma patient. Air Rescue Transport Helicopters like Dade County Fire and Rescue are subsidized by taxes and cost the residents of the county only what their insurance will pay. If they have no insurance, there is no cost to the patient. The Air Rescue Service provided by the Monroe County Fire Department recently implemented in the

Florida Keys cost taxpayers about fifty to sixty dollars per household on their property taxes.

In the first fifteen years of riding rescue and treating trauma patients, I watched many trauma patients die in route to the hospital because of the transport time. For example, on the 18 mile stretch south of Florida City on US Highway One, the transport time to the closest Trauma Center, Jackson Memorial Hospital in Miami, was an hour or more depending on traffic. It took the Air Rescue Helicopter six minutes to arrive on scene and fifteen minutes to load and transport to the same trauma unit, arriving within the golden hour. In my last fifteen years I saw many patients not only live, but recover fully and return to their family.

Chapter Thirty-two
HURRICANE ANDREW DEVASTATES HOMESTEAD AND FLORIDA CITY

It was August 25, 1992, and the hurricane season was nearing the peak period for storms. A small well-defined tropical storm developed on the coast of Africa and began tracking westerly toward the Bahamas and South Florida. This tropical storm became Hurricane Andrew just before reaching the eastern edge of the Bahamas. As it tracked on a westerly direction, it continued to grow finally reaching catastrophic proportions as it crossed over the Bahamas and into the warm waters of the gulf stream.

Andrew made landfall at Homestead/Florida City as a category five hurricane, with winds exceeding 200 miles per hour over a small area near the center of the storm and a storm surge of more than twenty feet. I was on duty at Metro Fire Station 36 in South Miami. I was assigned with nine other paramedics, six nurses and a thoracic surgeon from Jackson Memorial Hospital to a Hurricane Shelter just north of Homestead in South Miami. We had 3600 people in the shelter; lots of pregnant ladies, lots of people evacuated from the areas near the water. This Hurricane Shelter was a school built to stand the winds of a hurricane in 1985. It was a very sturdy building made of concrete and steel. Around 11:00 p.m. we began pulling our units off the street because of blinding rain and strong winds ahead of the storm.

My team and I entered the hurricane shelter bringing several field medical kits with all the equipment we might need during the storm, as there would be no going outside until the storm passed. We were prepared to do everything including surgery if needed during the storm. I rolled up in my bunker coat and boots and tried to get some rest, I knew after the storm there would be no time for resting. Luckily, we had a few medical emergencies during the night, all of them were simple. The full force of the storm would arrive around four o'clock in the morning. Andrew was a very intense storm but small in size not covering a large area. The hurricane force winds extended less than twenty miles out from the center of the storm. South Miami, Homestead and Florida City would bear the brunt of the intense winds around the center of the storm. Andrew was more like a very large tornado rather than a normal large hurricane.

At 5:00 o'clock in the morning the center of Hurricane Andrew passed over Homestead. Two men from the Homestead Air Force Base were forced to evacuate to our fire Station 16 in Homestead during the eye of the storm when their building was destroyed. They stated they had clocked winds of 216 miles per hour sustained and gusts of 250 miles per hour at the eye wall of the storm. Homestead Air Force Base was totally destroyed along with all of its equipment and planes. Our Hurricane Shelter held up pretty well for the first hour, then things started coming apart. Large Plexiglas domes over the stair wells (20 x 6 foot) designed to let light in to illuminate the stairs began to blow out from pressures inside the building. They were held in place by four inch by half inch steel straps bolted to the concrete roof. When they blew off, it sounded like ten sticks of dynamite going off. With the domes gone the stairwells filled with rock from the roof and rainwater rushed in. Water was about 12 inches deep in most of the school. We were like the fleet that came to stay in World War II, there was nowhere to go. We were certainly not going outside. After the storm passed, they discovered 25 openings in the roof the largest was 25 x 75 foot. But the building provided shelter, and no one was injured inside the building.

By 6:30 day light was breaking, and the hurricane winds had begun to subside. We were all crowded around the handheld police radio of one of the officers assigned to the shelter to hear the first reports from police cars now able to get on the road and begin to access the damage. "Oh My God," exclaimed one of the officers from the road, everything is on the ground. Concrete houses destroyed, roofs blown off, walls collapsed. Power poles were snapped off at ground level, even the big concrete poles were snapped off. Radio and TV towers on the ground. Thirty years of vegetation destroyed in less than two hours.

Most of the severe damage occurred from southwest 88th Street south to Florida City. The trailer parks looked like dumps, not one part of a trailer was recognizable, just twisted aluminum, insulation and rubble. Luckily people were smart enough to evacuate areas near the water and get out of trailers. As I listened to the reports coming in from the southwest section, I began thinking about the days ahead; no water supply, no electricity, very limited food supply, no toilets and thousands of people trapped in their houses by fallen trees.

In just several hours we were able to get back to our fire station and start running rescues; communications were poor at best. All our radio towers in the south end of the county were destroyed, the alarm office was using a ladder truck with an antenna zip tied to the top of the ladder. Unfortunately, our two rescue helicopters were left at Tamiami Airport during the storm, needless to say, they were not even usable for scrap medal. The helicopters were supposed to be flown out of harm's way to Palm Beach but for some reason they were not moved. One of the first emergencies other than the usual heart attacks, strokes and trauma emergencies, was patients in hospitals needing life-support systems. Emergency generators were breaking down, running out of fuel, etc.

We used a number of transport methods, on the ground with rescue trucks where roads were open and helicopter transport when needed. Calling for a helicopter was interesting--you might get anything from a black hawk to a huge army tank carrier or coast guard chopper. We transported patients north where power was available. Baptist Hospital on Kendal Drive handled the brunt of the emergencies. Baptist called in all their workers and had tee shirts printed and distributed to all there staff "Baptist Hospital, Ground Zero" Baptist is not only a great hospital but a spirited one as well.

The next challenge was flat tires, the streets were two feet deep in tiles from roofs and nails. We had to station a tire mechanic at every fire station to fix flat tires to keep the trucks moving. The next situation was people needing their prescribed medications, they were beginning to run out. The hospitals stocked us with lots of medications and we distributed them where needed while we were treating other patients. Then thousands of homeowners fired up tree saws and began cutting downed trees off of their house and cars. Most of these people had not used tree saws before, and I don't have to tell you what the next group of emergency injuries were. Roofers came in after the storm and began covering the roofs with plastic to keep the water out.

The next group of injuries were the roofers; many were not real experienced roofers. In the morning the plastic on one side of the roof would be covered with dew and the roofers would step over the crown of the roof onto the dew covered plastic and off the roof they would go. The plastic with dew on it was very slippery. Most falls from 18 feet or more are serious to fatal.

Finding addresses after the storm was very difficult, all of the normal landmarks were gone. All of the street signs were gone and covered up under trees and bushes. We would get close to an address and bail out of the truck and dig in the piles of tree limbs to find a street sign and then count streets to where we should turn.

Our disaster councilors warned us that about seventeen days after the storm people would begin to break down, and they were correct. Many had survived the storm under a mattress in the bathtub with no roof left on their house, lost most of their belongings and had to move in with several friends or relatives.

Some small incidents at the seventeen-day period would be the last straw on the camel's back and they would just lose it. Dogs biting dogs, kids fighting, two women in the same house, wow. Things slowly got better as electricity and water were restored to neighborhoods and people's lives started getting back to normal. In some areas of the south end of Dade County, it was six months before power was restored.

The workload was unbearable in the days after the storm. We were running double shifts and twice as much equipment as normal, but there was much to be done. We were running day and night and sleeping in the open area of the apparatus floor (where fire trucks are parked). Fire stations don't have windows and are normally air conditioned, sleeping inside the building was just too hot. On about the fourth day we returned to the station just after dark, and I saw a puzzling long line of emergency lights on the street near the station. As we got closer, I realized they were fire trucks, at least 10 or 12 of them. We pulled up alongside the long line of red trucks and stopped. A Captain from the lead truck walked over and introduced himself. All of these fire trucks were from Charleston, North Carolina and they were here to help us. We had assisted them after a devastating storm several years earlier, and they were here to repay the favor.

They came completely self-contained with food, water, tree saws, sleeping bags etc. They were a very welcome sight to very tired eyes. It would take months even years for south Dade County to come back and many areas were changed forever.

Chapter Thirty-three
LT. SHARPE RETIRES FROM THE METRO DADE FIRE DEPARTMENT

I was scheduled to retire from the fire department the year Hurricane Andrew struck but decided to stay on until February of 1993. I worked a lot of double shifts so my fellow firefighters could rebuild their houses and lives. It's funny, we always thought it would be me devastated by a hurricane. I continued after I retired to operate a big game offshore fishing business out of Summerland Key, called *Sea Boots* Charters. We are located just twenty miles east of Key West on the Overseas Highway US 1 and 89 miles north of the Island of Cuba.

Fishing was always my stress relief and I recommend it highly. The Florida Keys have certainly had their share of hurricanes with the extremely active hurricane seasons of the past ten years. Hurricane George in 1998 a category three storm passed over the Keys with 125 mile per hour sustained winds and gust up to 165 miles an hour. This storm pushed a nine-foot tidal surge from the ocean over the Keys and did millions of dollars' worth of damage. In 2005 Hurricane Wilma became a category one hurricane in the Caribbean Sea and within 14 hours strengthened into a category five storm packing sustained winds of 178 miles per hour with gusts over 200 miles per hour. Wilma was one of the strongest storms ever recorded. Luckily for Mexico and the Florida Keys this storm weakened into a category four storm making landfall in Cancun, Mexico as a category four hurricane with sustained winds of 140 miles per hour. Then moving just north of the Florida Keys as a category three storm bringing 125 mile an hour winds and a 13 foot tidal surge from the Gulf side of the Keys on the back side of the storm as it passed. Wilma did millions of dollars' worth of damage in the Keys. Our home on Cudjoe Key sustained very little damage, most of the damage came in the form of economic depression after the storms. I built our home on Cudjoe with lots of concrete and steel and elevated it to 12.5 feet above high water.

My father taught me well; our new house on Summerland Key is rated for wind loads of 175 miles per hour and built to withstand the one-hundred-year flood plain. With that said, we still evacuate to the mainland during storms and keep a close eye on the tropics during hurricane season.

Tight lines and good fishing!
Captain Jim Sharpe

www.ingramcontent.com/pod-product-compliance
Lightning Source LLC
Chambersburg PA
CBHW081002120626

46546CB00010B/2998

* 9 7 8 1 9 5 7 0 7 7 6 5 9 *

www.ingramcontent.com/pod-product-compliance
Lightning Source LLC
Chambersburg PA
CBHW081004120626

4654/6CB00010B/3003